To Mich...
All the Very Best

John x

PRESTON TO BLACKPOOL

including Fleetwood

John Matthews and Peter Fitton

Series editor Vic Mitchell

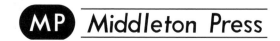

MP Middleton Press

Front cover: The photographer had balanced his tripod on a couple of stepladders to attain this image and, due to the gusty conditions, ended up with only two decent shots from a full roll of film! All is not what it appears here, on 27th October 2005. Black Five survivor no. 45407 masquerades as scrapped loco no. 44996 and is about to return to Rawtenstall on the East Lancashire Railway. (P.J.Fitton)

Back cover: Railway Clearing House map of 1947.

ACKNOWLEDGEMENTS

We are very grateful for the assistance received from many of those mentioned in the credits, also from the late R.M. Casserley, M.Claxton, G.Croughton, C.M.Howard, N.Langridge, D. and Dr S. Salter, Singleton History Group and M.Walmesley.

Published March 2018

ISBN 978 1 910356 16 6

© Middleton Press, 2018

Production Editor Deborah Esher
Design Cassandra Morgan
Cover design Matthew Esher

Published by
     Middleton Press
     Easebourne Lane
     Midhurst
     West Sussex
     GU29 9AZ
Tel: 01730 813169
Email: info@middletonpress.co.uk
www.middletonpress.co.uk

Printed and bound by CPI Group (UK) Ltd, Croydon, CR0 4YY

CONTENTS

INDEX

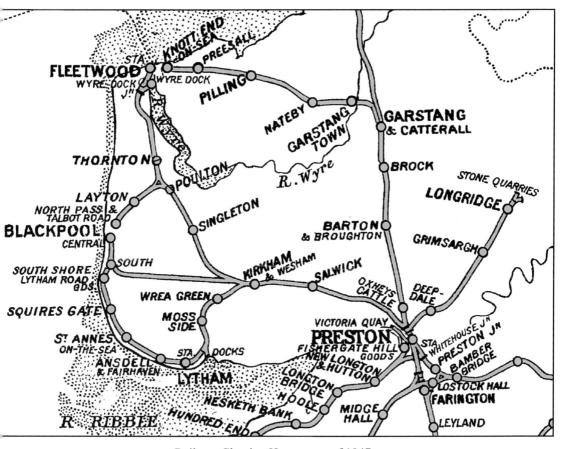

Railway Clearing House map of 1947.

GEOGRAPHICAL SETTING

The Fylde is a lowland coastal plain in West Lancashire. This roughly 13 square mile peninsula is bordered by the Irish Sea to the west, the Bowland Hills to the east, Morecambe Bay to the north and the River Ribble along its southern edge. The River Wyre makes its way through the Fylde, from Garstang on the eastern edge, westwards towards Poulton-le-Fylde before heading north to the sea at Fleetwood. It is an area of stark contrast, with the urban centres of Blackpool, St. Annes, Lytham and Fleetwood on the west coast, compared with large agricultural and rural areas centrally and over to the east. To say the Fylde is flat would be a great understatement, meaning there is a lack of notable engineering features. The M55 motorway leaves the M6 at Broughton, just north of Preston, and cuts through farmlands and countryside before running over a section of the now closed 'Marton'direct railway to central Blackpool.

The Fylde originally meant 'The Plain' and referred to the fairly level and largely marshy area between the River Wyre, near Fleetwood, and the River Ribble, near Lytham St. Annes. This area of southwest Lancashire had many coastal dunes, which attracted visitors. The underlying deposits are mostly red sandstones. The maps are to the scale of 25ins to 1 mile, with north at the top, unless otherwise indicated.

HISTORICAL BACKGROUND

The first proper railway to reach Preston arrived from the south in 1838. The North Union Railway opened up connections to the town from London, Birmingham, Manchester and Liverpool. To the north of the station was Maudlands, where the Preston & Wyre Railway line to Fleetwood opened on 15th July 1840 after Parliamentary approval had been granted in 1835. Maudlands was also where the Preston & Longridge Railway line joined the PWR by means of a level crossing over the main line. This was removed in 1885, when the PLR gained access to the main Preston station. Today, the point where the Blackpool line leaves the West Coast Main Line became known as Fylde Junction.

Soon, expansion of the Fylde's railways was under way, with the building of two new lines. The 4.75 mile Lytham branch left the Fleetwood line just north of Kirkham, while a 3.5 mile line ran to the north end of Blackpool from a triangle at Poulton-le-Fylde. Both of

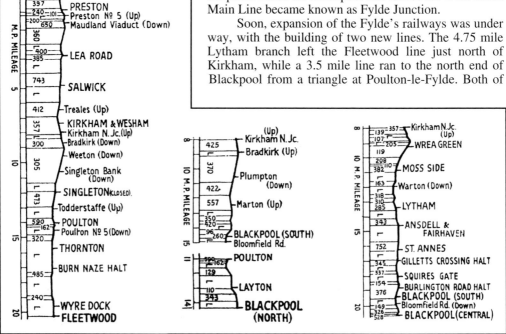

these railways opened in 1846, along with a short branch to Lytham Dock. In 1849, the PWR was taken over jointly by the Lancashire & Yorkshire and London North Western Railways. In 1861, a separate company, the Blackpool & Lytham Railway, started construction of a line from Lytham to Blackpool, which was opened on 6th April 1863. So, for eight years Lytham had two stations with no link between them, but in 1874 this was remedied, and also a direct line was constructed from Kirkham to Wrea Green. In 1903, a new line from Kirkham North Junction to Blackpool Waterloo Road (later South) was opened. Running directly via Marton, the line, with no intermediate stations, was used mainly for the ever increasing number of excursion and holiday trains.

All the Fylde lines became part of the London Midland & Scottish Railway in 1923 and this formed much of the London Midland Region of British Railways upon nationalisation in 1948. Blackpool Central closed on 2nd November 1964. The Fleetwood branch lost its passenger service on 1st June 1970. Freight closures are given in the captions.

Following privatisation North Western Trains commenced operation to Blackpool North and South on 2nd March 1997. This became First North Western in November 1998 and operated until 11th December 2004.

Virgin Cross Country operated services between Blackpool North and Portsmouth Harbour from May 1998 until May 2003. Virgin West Coast also ran limited services from Blackpool North to London Euston from May 1998 until May 2003 and again from December 2014.

From 12th December 2004, Northern operated services to a range of destinations, many of which are mentioned in the captions. Between 2004 and 2016, TransPennine Express operated services from Blackpool North to Manchester Airport. These transferred to Northern thereafter.

Closure for electrification work between Preston and Blackpool North took place on 11th November 2017. The Blackpool South service recommenced on 29th January 2018 and the Kirkham-North route reopened on 25th March of that year. The signal boxes on both routes were replaced by a new signalling system comprising 84 new colour light signals, controlled from Network Rail's Manchester Rail Operating Centre.

PASSENGER SERVICES

As the network expanded, passenger numbers increased dramatically, with new stations springing up at Bispham, later named Layton, Lea, Salwick and Weeton. Until 1848, the principal route from London to Glasgow was via the PWR, with a sea crossing linking Fleetwood and Ardrossan. A great improvement for passengers came from 1844, when the PWR trains started running into Preston's North Union station and beyond; thus weary travellers no longer had to alight at the PWR Maudland station and walk the half mile between the two.

Besides the regular Preston to Blackpool service, from 1899 an additional curve at Poulton, complete with its own halt, was laid allowing frequent trains between Blackpool and Fleetwood, later operated by LYR steam railmotors. Excursion and holiday trains brought many thousands of people for a day, or even longer to the seaside. Specials, run by large companies to take their workers away for the day, were also regular visitors to the resort. In 1896, for example, 17 trains, carrying nearly 11,000 day trippers, were organised by Bass Breweries from Burton on Trent. Even after rationalisation of the Fylde's railways, holiday specials ran well into the 1980s. These summer services arrived from many parts of the country, including Glasgow, Newcastle, Leicester, Chesterfield and Leeds, not forgetting Stranraer. The captions reveal others.

On the next two pages are examples of Victorian services. The timetable for June 1960 showed up departures Mondays to Fridays thus: (Saturday are in bold and Sundays in brackets). Fleetwood inland 15 **20** (8), Fleetwood to Blackpool North 27 **29** (8), Blackpool North inland 12 **27** (8) and Blackpool Central inland 54 **59** (7).

In 2017, four trains per hour linked Preston and Blackpool North, while there was an hourly service to Blackpool South.

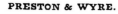

PRESTON & WYRE.   Sec. & Su. H. B. Jones ·

Preston to Fleetwood, 10 a.m.   4 and 7 ¼ m.

Fleetwood to Preston, Liverpool, Manchester,
&c., 7 & 9 a.m. 3¼ & 6 p.m.; to **London**, 9 a.m. and 3 30 p.m.

On Sundays,
Preston to Fleetwood 8¼ a.m.

Fleetwood to Preston, Liverpool, Manchester,
London, &c., at 3 30 p.m.

From Bolton to Fleetwood—On SUNDAYS, at 8 a.m.

From Liverpool to Fleetwood, 8 a.m., 2¼ and 4 30
p.m. mixed. On SUNDAYS, at 7 30 a.m.

From Manchester to Fleetwood, (Victoria station,)
8½, a.m., 2½ and 4¾ p.m. mixed.

From the New Bailey-street Station,
On SUNDAYS, at 8 a.m.

FARES—Fleetwood to Preston (North Union Station), 1st class,
4s.; 2nd. class, 3s.; 3rd, class 2s.; to Poulton, 1s.—9d.—6d.;
to Kirkham, 3s.—2s.—1s. 6d ; to Chorley, 6s. 6d.—4s. 6d.—3s.;
to Bolton, 8s.—6s.—4s.; to Manchester, via Bolton, 10s.—7s. 6d.
—5s.; to Liverpool, 11s. 6d.—8s.

From London to Fleetwood, 6 and 10 a.m., 1st class,
and 8½ p.m. mail.

FARES.—Passengers to London, first class, £3 1s. 6d.; second
class, £2 0s. 6d. Carriages, 4 wheels, £8 5s., 2 wheels, £7.
One horse, £5 12s 6d.; two, £9 9s; three, £12 8s.

Bradshaw, January 1845

Bradshaw, June 1876

FLEETWOOD, BLACKPOOL, LYTHAM, PRESTON, CHORLEY, BOLTON, and MANCHESTER.—L. & Y.—West.

[Large railway timetable grid with columns for Week Days and Sundays, showing stations including Dock Street Station, Fleetwood, Cleveleys, Poulton Junction, Blackpool (Talbot d), Bispham, Poulton Junc., Singleton, Kirkham Junc., Lytham, Moss Side, Wrea Green, Salwick, Lea Road, Preston, Birmingham, London (Euston), Glasgow, Edinburgh, Carlisle, Windermere, Kendal, Whitehaven, Furness Abbey, Ulverston, Lancaster, Preston, Farrington, Leyland, Euxton, Chorley, Adlington, Blackrod & Horwich J., Lostock Lane, Lostock Jn., Bolton, Moses Gate, Farnworth, Stoneclough, Dixon Fold, Clifton Junction, Pendleton, Salford, Manchester.]

BLACKPOOL and LYTHAM (Coast Route).—Preston and Wyre.

[Timetable with stations: Hounds Hill Blackpool, South Shore, St. Annes, Ansdell, Lytham.]

FLEETWOOD, BLACKPOOL, LYTHAM, PRESTON, CHORLEY, and MANCHESTER.—Lancashire and Yorkshire.

Up. — **Week Days**—*Continued on opposite page.*

For other Trains, see page 476. Arrivals, Local Trains, page 471.

Steamer leaves	mrn	aft	mrn	mrn	mrn	mrn	mrn	mrn	mrn	mrn	mrn
Belfast		8c0									
Douglas (Isle of Man)		mrn									
Fleetwd (train) dp		6 30			7 10		7 53	7 53			
Cleveleys		Mn.			7 18		8 2	8 2			
Poulton arr.					7 23		8 6	8 6			
Blackpool* dep.			7 5		7 10			8 20			8 12
Bispham					7 14						
Poulton arr.					7 19			8 26			8 19
Poulton dep.		Mn.			7 27		8 7	8 27			8 20
Singleton							8 12				
Kirkham arr.					7 38		8 21				8 31
Blackpool† dep.	6 5			7 20		7 25	7 57		8 15	8 20	
South Shore	6 9			7 25		7 29	8 1		8 20	8 24	
St. Annes	6 16	Belfast Boat Train.	Mondays only.			7 36	8 7	Except Saturdays.		8 31	
Ansdell						7 40	8 11				
Lytham arr	6 22					7 43	8 14			8 36	
Lytham dep	6 23					7 46	8 15			8 37	
Moss Side											
Wrea Green	6 32										
Kirkham arr.	6 36						8 25				
Kirkham dep.	6 38				7 41		8 27				8 34
Salwick [304, 465	6 44				7 47						8 40
Lea Road [486, 488,	6 49				7 52						8 45
Preston 262, 302, arr	6 55	7 0			7 58	8 6	8 42				8 51
312 Manchester ‡ arr	Stop				10 8						10g6
534 Glasgow (Cen.) dp				Runs on the 8th, 14th, 21st, and 28th instant.			To E. L. District.		Runs on the 8th, 14th, 21st, and 28th instant only.		
534 Edinbro' (P.St.)											
304 Carlisle (Cit.)											
307 Windermere §			Via Atherton.					Via Atherton.			
Kendal 307											7 10
309 Whitehaven											
309 Barrow (Cen.)											
309 Windrmre (L.S)											
Ulverston 309											
304 Lancastr (Cas.)	mrn				7 10		mrn				7 56
Preston dep.	7 23	7 5			8 9		8 12				9 2
Farington	7 29										
Leyland	7 34						8 21				
Euxton	7 39										
Chorley 471, 470	7 46	7 21		Via Atherton.			8 30		Via Atherton.		9 19
Adlington	7 53						8 36				
Blackrod 464	7 58						8 41				
Lostock Jn. 466, 478	8 4						8 47				
Bolton 479	8 12	7 40			8b39		8 54			9b25	9 41
Moses Gate	8 24										
Farnworth ‖	8 26										
Stoneclough	8 29										
Dixon Fold	8 33										
Clifton Junc.	8 37										
Pendleton	8 42										
Salford	8 46	7 56	8 11	8 40	8 55		9 9	9 26	9 36	9 41	9 58
Manchester	8 50	8 0	8 15	8 45	9 0		9 13	9 30	9 40	9 45	10 3

Steamer leaves	mrn	mrn	mrn	mrn	mrn	mrn	mrn	mrn	mrn	mrn	mrn
Belfast											
Douglas (Isle of Man)									8 30	8 30	
Fleetwd (train) dp	8 25	8 40			9 58	Thro' Train to Bradford and Leeds, via Burnley.	1027	1130	1220	1230	
Cleveleys	8 34	8 49			10 [illegible]		1036	1139			
Poulton arr.	8 38	8 53			1012		1040	1143			
Blackpool* dep.		8 40			1010		1035	1140	Waits the arrival of the Isle of Man Steamer.		
Bispham		8 44						1145			
Poulton arr.		8 49			1017		1043	1150			
Poulton dep.	8 39	8 57			1018		1048	1154			
Singleton					1024		1053	1159			
Kirkham arr.	8 50	9 8			1033		11 2	12 8		1249	
Blackpool† dep.	8 27		8 55	9 0		10 7	1020	1125		1210	
South Shore	8 31		8 59	9 4		1012	1026	1130		1215	
St. Annes	8 37		9 5	9 10	L. & N. W. Train.	1019	1033	1137		1222	
Ansdell							1037	1141			
Lytham arr	8 43		9 11	9 16		1026	1040	1145		1228	
Lytham dep	8 44		9 13	9 17		1028	1043	1147		1229	
Moss Side	8 49						1048	1152			
Wrea Green	8 53						1052	1156			
Kirkham arr.	8 57			9 27		1040	1057	12 1		1240	
Kirkham dep.	8 59	9 11		9 30	1035	1043	11 7	1213		1253	
Salwick [304, 465		9 17				1049		1219			
Lea Road [486, 488,		9 22				1054		1224			
Preston 262, 302, arr	9 12	9 28	9 33	9 43	1050	11 0	1122	1230		1 6	
312 Manchester ‡ arr	1030	1030	1030		1155	1241		2 0		2 50	
534 Glasgow (Cen.) dp	Stop					Stop					
534 Edinbro' (P.St.)											
304 Carlisle (Cit.)				6 50			8 40			To East Lancashire and Yorkshire Districts. Waits the arrival of the Isle of Man Steamer.	
307 Windermere §				[illegible] 10			9 20				1115
Kendal 307				[illegible]			9 40				1129
309 Whitehaven							6 55				
309 Barrow (Cen.)			To East Lancashire District.	7a0			8 55				10 5
309 Windrmre (L.S)				7g45			8 35				9 53
Ulverston 309				7 31	a		9 26				1027
304 Lancastr (Cas.)	mrn			9 0		mrn	1038				1216
Preston dep.	9 4			9 47		1130	1125	1235			1255
Farington	9 9					1136					1 1
Leyland	9 14					1141	1134				1 6
Euxton						1146					1 11
Chorley 471, 470	9 23			10 3		1153	1144	1251			1 18
Adlington	9 29			d		12 0					1 24
Blackrod 464	9 34					12 6					1 29
Lostock Jn. 466, 478	9 40					1212					1 35
Bolton 479	9 47			1025		1219	12 4	1 11	1b20		1 42
Moses Gate	9 52					1224	1210				1 54
Farnworth ‖	9 54					1226					Change at Bolton.
Stoneclough						1229					
Dixon Fold						1233					
Clifton Junc.						1237					
Pendleton						1242					
Salford	10 6			1043		1246	1222	1 28	1 35		2 6
Manchester	1010			1048		1250	1227	1 33	1 40		2 10

Steamer leaves	aft	aft	aft	aft	aft	aft	aft	aft	aft	aft	aft
Belfast											
Douglas (Isle of Man)											
Fleetwd (train) dp		1 17				2 25				3 10	
Cleveleys		1 26				2 34				3 19	
Poulton arr.		1 30				2 38				3 23	
Blackpool* dep.		1 20		Via Atherton.	2 20	2 35			2 45	3 20	
Bispham											
Poulton arr.		1 27			2 26	2 42			2 53	3 27	
Poulton dep.		1 33			2 28	2 46			2 55	3 31	
Singleton		1 38									
Kirkham arr.		1 47			2 39	2 57			3 6	3 42	
Blackpool† dep.		1 20	1 35	2 5		2 10	2 40	2 50		2 57	3 30
South Shore		1 25	1 42	2 12		2 17	2 47	2 57		3 4	3 37
St. Annes		1 32	1 49	2 19	L. & N. W. Train.	2 24	2 54	3 4	L. & N. W. Train.	3 11	3 44
Ansdell		1 36				2 28				3 15	
Lytham arr		1 39	1 55	2 25		2 31	3 0	3 10		3 18	3 50
Lytham dep		1 41	2 0	2 28		2 34	3 5	3 13		3 20	3 55
Moss Side										3 25	
Wrea Green										3 29	
Kirkham arr.		1 52				2 46				3 34	
Kirkham dep.		1 57			2 42	3 2			3 9	3 47	
Salwick [304, 465				Except Wednesdays and Thursdays.				Except Wednesdays and Thursdays.		3 53	
Lea Road [486, 488,										3 59	
Preston 262, 302, arr		2 10	2 20		2 55	3 15	Through Train to Huddersfield, Wakefield, &c., via Burnley.		3 23	4 5	Through Train to Bradford and Leeds, via Burnley.
312 Manchester ‡ arr		3 53	3 53						4 20	6 17	
534 Glasgow (Cen.) dp		10 0							Stop	1010	
534 Edinbro' (P.St.)		1015								1020	
304 Carlisle (Cit.)		1223				1234				1 40	
307 Windermere §			To East Lancashire and Yorkshire Districts.			1 35				2 20	
Kendal 307						1 52				2 40	
309 Whitehaven						1125					
309 Barrow (Cen.)						1 0				1 50	
309 Windrmre (L.S)						1255				1 40	
Ulverston 309						1 18				2 17	
304 Lancastr (Cas.)		1228				2 1			aft	3 27	
Preston dep.		2 15				3 18			4 27	4 10	
Farington									4 33		
Leyland									4 38	4 19	
Euxton									4 43		
Chorley 471, 470	2 0	2 31				3 35		Via Atherton.	4 50	4 29	
Adlington	2 6								4 57		
Blackrod 464	2 12								5 2		
Lostock Jn. 466, 478	2 18								5 8		
Bolton 479	2 25	2 51				3 55			5 15	4 48	
Moses Gate	2 34								5 29	4 54	
Farnworth ‖	2 36								5 31		
Stoneclough	2 39								5 34		
Dixon Fold									5 38		
Clifton Junc.	2 45								5 42		
Pendleton	2 50					4 11			5 47		
Salford	2 54	3 6		3 30		4 15		4 18	5 51	5 6	
Manchester	2 58	3 10		3 35		4 20		4 23	5 55	5 10	

a Leaves Barrow (Central) at 7 50 and Ulverston at 8 8 mrn. on Mondays. **b** Stop to set down only.
c Except Sunday nights. **d** Stops to take up for Manchester. **g** Mondays only.
* Talbot Road Station. † Central Station. ‡ Exchange Station, *via* Tyldesley. § L. & N. W. ‖ Farnworth and Halshaw Moor.

Up—*Continued.* — **Week Days**—*Continued from page 474.* — **Sundays.**

For other Trains, see page 476. Arrivals, Local Trains, page 471.

Steamer leaves	aft	aft	aft	aft	aft	aft	aft	aft	aft	aft	aft
Belfast											
Douglas (Isle of Man)											
Fleetwood (train) d					4 47					6 0	
Cleveleys					4 56					6 9	
Poulton					5 0					6 13	
Blackpool * dep.	4 0		4 35		4 55		5 15	5 50			6 35
Bispham					5 0						
Poulton arr.					5 5		5 22				6 42
Poulton dep.					5 10		5 24			6 14	6 44
Singleton					5 15						
Kirkham arr.	4 18				5 23		5 35			6 26	6 55
Blackpool † dep.		3 55		4 30	4 40	5 0				6 0	
South Shore		4 2		4 37	4 47	5 7				6 7	
St. Annes	L. & N. W. Train.	4 9		4 44	4 54	5 14	L. & N. W. Train.			6 14	L. & N. W. Train.
Ansdell					4 58						
Lytham arr.		4 15		4 50	5 1	5 20				6 20	
Lytham dep.		4 20		4 53	5 3	5 23				6 22	
Moss Side					5 8						
Wrea Green					5 12						
Kirkham arr.					5 17					6 33	
Kirkham dep.	4 20				5 30		5 38			6 37	6 57
Salwick					5 36						
Lea Road [489, 305, 465					5 42						
Preston 264, 302, 487, a	4 35	4 40			5 50		5 53			6 50	7 10
312 Manchester ‡.. arr.	5 33						7 6				Stop
536 Glasgow (Cen.) dep.				Through Train to Bradford, Cleckheaton Branch, and Dewsbury, via Burnley.	1010				2 0		
536 Edinbro' (P.St.)					1020				2 0		
305 Carlisle (Citadel)					1 50				4 22		
307 Windermere §			Via Atherton.		3 15			Via Atherton.	4 25		
Kendal 307					3 33				4 42		
309 Whitehaven	Except Wednesdays and Thursdays.	To East Lancashire District.							2 55	To East Lancashire District.	
309 Barrow (Central)					2 5[illegible]				4 25		
309 Windermere (LS)					2 59				4 15		
Ulverston 309.					3 21				4 43		aft
305 Lancaster (Cstle)					4 39				5 27		7 0
Preston dep.					5 57				6 28		7 33
Farington					6 3						
Leyland					6 8						
Euxton											
Chorley 471, 470			Through Train to Stalybridge.		6 18			Through Train to Oldham.	6 44		7 49
Adlington					6 25						
Blackrod 464					6 31						
Lostock Junc. 467, 478					6 38						
Bolton 479					6 50	6e11			7 2		8 10
Moses Gate					6 58						
Farnworth ‖											Mons. & Sats.
Stoneclough									Via Prestwich.		
Dixon Fold											
Clifton Jnction.											
Pendleton					7 10						
Salford			5 45		7 15	6 27		7 3			8 26
Manchester..ar			5 50		7 20	6 32		7 8	7 27		8 30

Steamer leaves	aft	aft	aft	aft	aft	aft	aft	aft	aft	aft
Belfast										
Douglas (Isle of Man)										
Fleetwood (train) d			Through Train to Bury, Heywood, & Rochdale.	7 0		8 25		9 50		
Cleveleys				7 9		8 34		9 59		
Poulton				7 13		8 38		10 3		
Blackpool * dep.		7 0		7 10		8 35		10 0	1015	1030
Bispham				7 15		8 40				Sat.
Poulton arr.		7 7		7 19		8 44		10 7		1037
Poulton dep.		7 9		7 24		8 48		10 8		1038
Singleton										
Kirkham arr.		7 20		7 35		8 59		1019		1049
Blackpool † dep.	6 45		6 50			8 15	8 45			1010
South Shore	6 52		6 57			8 20	8 51			1015
St. Annes	6 59	L. & N. W. Train.	7 4			8 27	8 58		Saturdays only.	1022
Ansdell						8 31				
Lytham arr.	7 5		7 10			8 34	9 4			1028
Lytham dep.	7 7		7 13			8 36	9 5			1030
Moss Side						8 41				
Wrea Green			7 20			8 45				1037
Kirkham arr.			7 25			8 50	9 17			1042
Kirkham dep.		7 22	7 28	7 39		9 4	9 21	1022		1052
Salwick						9 10				d
Lea Road [489, 305, 465						9 16				d
Preston 264, 302, 487, a		7 35	7 41	7 52		9 22	9 34	1035		11 5
312 Manchester ‡.. arr.			8 58	8 58		11 3				
536 Glasgow (Cen.) dep.										5 50
536 Edinbro' (P.St.)										6 0
305 Carlisle (Citadel)				5 38						8 41
307 Windermere §				6 0	6f45	6 50				9 0
Kendal 307		Mondays and Saturdays. Will not run after the 26th instant.		6 45	7f3	7 12				9 18
309 Whitehaven							To East Lancashire District.			7 30
309 Barrow (Central)				5 40						9 0
309 Windermere (LS)				5 40						8 35
Ulverston 309.				6 11						9 21
305 Lancaster (Cstle)				7 21	7f50	8 18				10 4
Preston dep.			7 43	8 0	8 40	9 27				1110
Farington					8 46					
Leyland					8 51					1119
Euxton					8 56					
Chorley 471, 470	Via Atherton.		8 0	8 16	9 2	9 43			11 0	1129
Adlington					9 8	9 50				
Blackrod 464					9 13	9 56				
Lostock Junc. 467, 478					9 19	10 2				
Bolton 479			8 20	8 36	9 27	1010			1120	1149
Moses Gate					9 34	1017				
Farnworth ‖					9 36					
Stoneclough					9 40					
Dixon Fold					9 43					
Clifton Jnction.					9 47					
Pendleton				8 50	9 52					
Salford	8 8			8 55	9 56	1030			1136	12 5
Manchester..ar	8 12			9 0	10 0	1035			1140	1210

Sundays.

Steamer leaves	mrn	aft	aft	aft	aft	aft	aft	aft	aft	aft	aft
Belfast	8a0										
Douglas (Isle of Man)											
Fleetwood (train) d	7 20	1 35			5 10				7 30		
Cleveleys	7 29	1 44			5 19				7 39		
Poulton	7 33	1 48			5 23				7 43		
Blackpool * dep.	7 25	1 40			5 15				7 35		9 0
Bispham	7 30	1 45			5 20				7 40		
Poulton arr.	7 36	1 51			5 26				7 46		
Poulton dep.	7 40	1 53			5 29				7 50		
Singleton											
Kirkham arr.	7 51	2 4			5 40				8 1		
Blackpool † dep.	7 10	1 20	2 0	4 55	4 55	6 35	7 5	7 20		8 50	
South Shore	7 14	1 25	2 5	5 0	5 0	6 40	7 10	7 25		8 55	
St. Annes	7 21	1 32	2 12	5 7	5 7	6 47	7 17	7 32		9 2	
Ansdell	7 25	1 36		5 11	5 11		7 21				
Lytham arr.	7 28	1 39	2 18	5 14	5 14	6 53	7 24	7 38		9 8	
Lytham dep.	7 30	1 42	2 20	5 17	5 17	6 55	7 26	7 40		9 12	
Moss Side	7 35	1 47		5 22	5 22		7 31				
Wrea Green	7 39	1 51		5 26	5 26		7 35				
Kirkham arr.	7 44	1 56	2 31	5 31	5 31	7 6	7 40	7 52			
Kirkham dep.	7 55	2 7	2 34	5 35	5 45	7 9	7 43	7 55	8 5		
Salwick	8 2	2 13			5 52				8 12		
Lea Road [489, 305, 465	8 8	2 19			5 58				8 18		
Preston 264, 302, 487, a	8 15	2 25	2 47	5 50	6 5	7 22	7 57	8 8	8 25	9 32	
312 Manchester ‡.. arr.	1031				8 23						
536 Glasgow (Cen.) dep.											
536 Edinbro' (P.St.)											
305 Carlisle (Citadel)									4 30		
307 Windermere §			To East Lancashire District.			To East Lancashire and Yorkshire Districts.			5 45	To East Lancashire District.	
Kendal 307									6 7		
309 Whitehaven									8b33		
309 Barrow (Central)									4 45		
309 Windermere (LS)									4 45		
Ulverston 309.									5 16		
305 Lancaster (Cstle)	7 10								7 13		
Preston dep.	8 25	2 30		5 55	6 17			8 12	8 30		
Farington	8 32	2 37			6 24				8 37		
Leyland	8 37	2 42		6 5	6 29			8 21	8 42		
Euxton	8 42	2 47			6 34				8 47		
Chorley 471, 470	8 50	2 54		6 15	6 41			8 31	8 55		
Adlington	8 57	3 1		6 23	6 49			8 38	9 3		
Blackrod 464	9 3	3 7		6 29	6 55			8 44	9 10		
Lostock Junc. 467, 478	9 10	3 14		6 35	7 2			8 51	9 17		
Bolton 479	9 18	3 23		6 45	7 12			9 0	9 27		10e0
Moses Gate	9 24	3 29			7 19			9 6	9 34		
Farnworth ‖									9 36		
Stoneclough	9 29								9 39		
Dixon Fold											
Clifton Jnction.									9 46		
Pendleton	9c37	3c40		7c1	7c30			9c17	9c51		
Salford	9 41	3 44		7 5	7 34			9 21	9 55		1015
Manchester..ar	9 47	3 50		7 10	7 40			9 27	10 0		1020

a Leaves Belfast on Saturday night. **b** Morning Train from Whitehaven. **c** New Station (Broad Street). **d** Stops when required to set down from Blackpool.
e Stop to set down only. **f** Mondays only.
* Talbot Road. † Central Station. ‡ Exchange Station, *via* Tyldesley. § L. & N. W. ‖ Farnworth and Halshaw Moor.

Bradshaw, August 1893

1. Preston to Blackpool Central

PRESTON

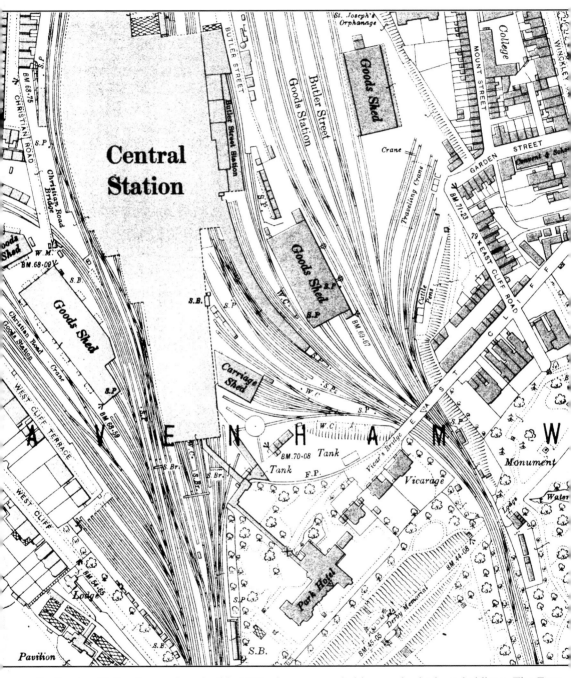

I. Preston Station is seen here in this 1931 view surrounded by goods sheds and sidings. The East Lancashire line, starting from its own platforms on the Butler Street side of the station, is running off towards Bamber Bridge at the bottom right of the map. Another point of interest is the former L&YR and LNWR jointly owned Park Hotel, with its covered walkway directly into the station, as well as the Vicar's Bridge, which still survived in 2018.

1. We start our journey at Preston station with this view looking south around 1900. We are on the main down platform, no. 5, which is now no. 3, but all was still easily recognisable in 2018. (P.Laming coll.)

2. The original North Union station, dating from 1838, had become inadequate for the growing levels of traffic. Major improvements, with additional lines and platforms were undertaken, and the new station opened on 21st September 1879. Around 1900 we look south again, this time from the original platform no. 2. Here, a Horwich-built L&YR 2-4-2 Radial Tank waits on the through road before taking a train to Blackpool North. The roof covering this part of the station was removed in about 1958. (P.Laming coll.)

3. Seen at the south end of the station, in the mid-1930s, a good selection of LNWR signals controls the approaching lines. Heading out of the station with two wagons is ex-L&YR 2-4-2 station pilot no. 10639, with the extensive Christian Road goods depot and sidings behind. A long time Preston loco, built at Horwich Works in 1890, it was withdrawn in May 1952. The locally named 'Glass Bridge' can be seen on the far right; this provided a direct link to the main platforms from the nearby Park Hotel. (LOSA)

From *Good Lines*, the monthly journal of the Temperance Society, dated 1911.

4. Pictured at no. 3 platform on 22nd July 1961 is a service for Blackpool headed by class 4 2-6-4T no. 42476, which, during its final time in service, was based at Lostock Hall. This platform is now no. 1 and is still similar in appearance today, although the photographer's vantage point is no longer available. (P.Claxton)

5. This classic view of Preston station is from 1st September 1963. The train is a Euston to Carlisle service in the capable hands of Britannia class 4-6-2 no. 70054 *Dornoch Firth*. The engine had emerged from Crewe Works in September 1954 and survived until withdrawal from Carlisle Kingmoor on the 26th November 1966. (P.Claxton)

6. Class B1 4-6-0 no.61115, built by the North British Locomotive Company, is seen passing through the East Lancs side platform no. 8 with a Leeds Central to Blackpool Central working on 30th May 1964. These 4-6-0s were welcome visitors to the area, bringing in holidaymakers from West Yorkshire and further afield in the 1950s and 60s. (P.J.Fitton)

7. On the same day we have a good view of the extensive track work and signalling just to the south of the station. Racing north, both trains are heading for Blackpool Central. To the left, class 5 4-6-0 no. 45188, has travelled over the Pennines from Huddersfield, while classmate no. 45312 has had an easy run on the main line from Wigan. The latter 4-6-0, one of 842 built, was based at Bolton, when it retired as late as June 1968. (P.J.Fitton)

8. Built at Derby in February 1967, this BR Type 2 loco first appeared as no. D7672 before later becoming no. 25322. Pictured here on 18th May 1985, when carrying the name *Tamworth Castle*, it is unusually working the 07.20 Blackpool North to Cambridge service. Renumbered later as no. 25912, it ran until September 1991 and fortunately it was saved before the cutter's torch got to work, and in 2017 was awaiting restoration at the Churnet Valley Railway. (J.Matthews)

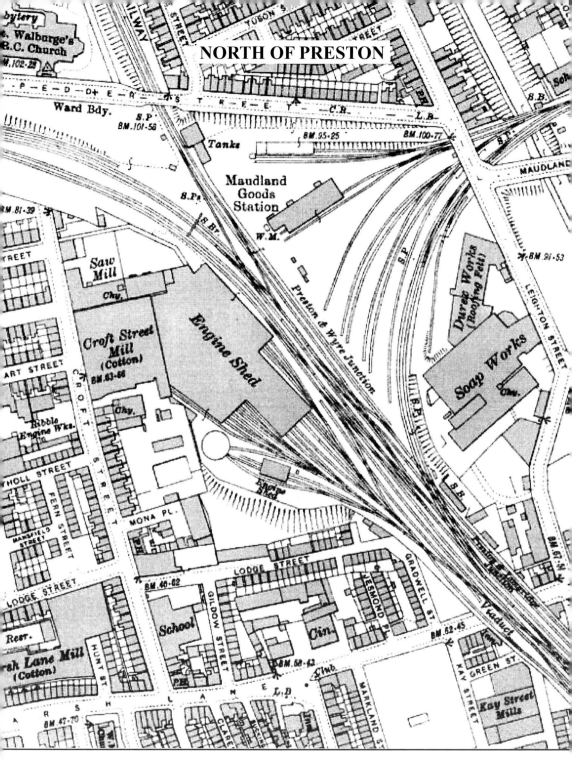

II. Moving to the northern end of Preston, here is a 1930 view showing the Maudlands area. Cotton mills predominate, with the Longridge line branching off to the right and Maudland Goods Station, the site of the original P&WR station. The line to the Fylde sweeps to the left.

9. Now we are heading north out of the station with a superb panorama ahead, looking from the cab of a Fleetwood allocated BR Class 2 Standard 2-6-2T, the photograph being taken by the driver. Numbered 84000 to 84029, these 30 locos were introduced from 1953, with this class member heading for Blackpool Central in 1964. What remains of the former Preston shed can be seen centre left, along with the unmistakeable St. Walburge's Church steeple, which at 94m is the tallest for a Parish Church in England. (T.Bretherton)

10. Another splendid view is looking towards Maudlands and the junction with the Longridge Branch. The goods facilities here survived until 1981, but the Maudland Bridge station and the flat crossing on the main line saw early closure in 1885. The goods warehouse can be picked out on the left, as a class 9F 2-10-0 heads north with a heavy freight for Carlisle, passing the ex-LNWR Preston No.5 box in August 1967. (L.Nixon)

↑ 11. On the bright morning of 23rd December 1962, class 4 2-6-4T no. 42154 heads a Blackpool bound parcels train past Maudlands. Of interest is the first van behind the loco, which is a six-wheel LNWR stores van. (P.Claxton)

↗ 12. Resting at their home shed on 26th April 1949 are class 3F 0-6-0T no. 47291 and behind it Radial Tank no. 10676. The former was built in 1924, while the still LMS numbered 2-4-2T engine was a Horwich product of 1892. The shed itself came to a premature end on 28th June 1960, when a fire destroyed the roof beyond repair, and although staff valiantly soldiered on in terrible conditions, it finally closed on 12th September 1961. The coaling tower is on the left. (H.C.Casserley)

→ 13. Here is a chance meeting at Fylde Junction on 16th December 1967, with the long closed shed to the left. The photographer has caught this stunning image of a class 47 diesel hauling a southbound passenger train from Blackpool, as class 5 4-6-0 no. 45350 takes the Blackpool line with a coal train for Wyre Dock. (L.Nixon)

14. A little further along the Blackpool line at Maudlands, and overlooked by St. Mark's Church, a class 40 hauled empty oil train from Burn Naze meets APT set no. 370002. These troubled sets were on trial along the WCML at the time of this picture, 11th November 1979, and this one expired just north of Preston. Station pilot class 08 no. 08744 was brought in to rescue the train, and here it is being inspected by rail staff and engineers. (J.Matthews)

15. Perched on stilts at the eastern end of Maudland Viaduct, the 1889 Railway Signal Company box of the same name stands guard as class 5 4-6-0 no. 45271 heads the 12.40 Blackpool Central to Manchester Victoria service on 1st September 1964. The closure of the signal box came in February 1973. (P.J.Fitton)

16. The extremely flat nature of the Fylde lines means a scarcity of engineering features. One exception is the 10-arched Maudland Viaduct, opened in July 1840 carrying a single line, which was doubled in 1846. Further expansion came later when the L&YR quadrupled the lines between Preston and Kirkham. On 1st July 2017, no. 37025 heads west across the viaduct with a special charter train from Edinburgh. In fact, this was the final loco hauled passenger train to visit Blackpool North before electrification. The engine, seen in large logo livery, was built at the Vulcan Foundry in August 1961, appearing as D6725. (J.Matthews)

17. On the outskirts of Preston was Ashton signal box, dating from 1879. Its original frame was replaced by a new 18 lever one in 1889, and closed on 4th February 1973. A little before closure, on the now double track, a Blackpool to Leeds class 110 DMU heads for Preston. (P.J.Fitton)

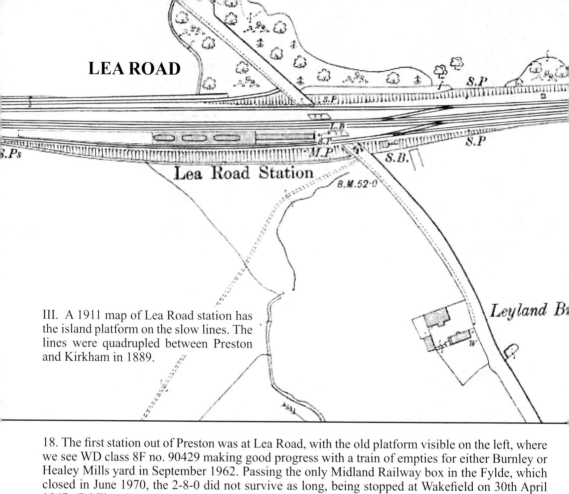

LEA ROAD

Lea Road Station

III. A 1911 map of Lea Road station has
the island platform on the slow lines. The
lines were quadrupled between Preston
and Kirkham in 1889.

18. The first station out of Preston was at Lea Road, with the old platform visible on the left, where
we see WD class 8F no. 90429 making good progress with a train of empties for either Burnley or
Healey Mills yard in September 1962. Passing the only Midland Railway box in the Fylde, which
closed in June 1970, the 2-8-0 did not survive as long, being stopped at Wakefield on 30th April
1967. (P.J.Fitton)

↑　19. Opened in 1842 by the Preston & Wyre Railway, the station at Lea Road survived until closure on 2nd May 1938. Pictured on the four track section heading for Blackpool, on 22nd September 1962, is a Batchelors Works special, in the hands of Jubilee class 4-6-0 no. 45701 *Conqueror*. (P.J.Fitton)

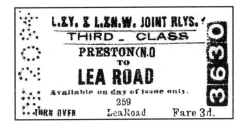

EAST OF SALWICK

20. Between Lea Road and Salwick stations stood the isolated Constable Lane signal box. A 14-lever L&YR design, built in 1897, it was closed on 28th June 1970. Sadly, on 15th November of the same year, we take a last look as the demolition gang gets to work. Passing the scene is a class 50 heading a Blackpool to Euston service, with debris both sides of the track and Springfields Works visible in the distance. (P.J.Fitton)

L. & Y. & L. & N. W. JOINT RLYS.
Issued subject to the regulations & conditions in
the Co's Time Tables, Books, Bills, and Notices,
Available on day of issue only.

THIRD CLASS
LEA ROAD
TO
PRESTON
26C
PRESTON   fare 3d

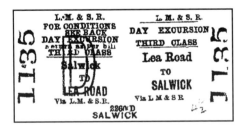

L.M. & S.R.   L.M. & S.R.
FOR CONDITIONS   DAY EXCURSION
SEE BACK
DAY EXCURSION   THIRD CLASS
THIRD CLASS   Lea Road
Salwick   TO
TO
LEA ROAD   SALWICK
Via L.M. & S.R.   Via L.M & S.R
2260 D
SALWICK

L. & N.W.R.   L. & N.W.R.
Available on day of issue   PLEASURE PARTY
only. Not transferable   (Local Series)
PLEASURE PARTY   OUTWARD HALF
RETURN HALF   Third Class (Parly)
Third Class (Parly)   Lea Road
TO
on L. & N. W. Ry. To
LEA ROAD   on L. & N. W. Ry.
Via   Via
Turn over) 897(LPP)   Fare s d

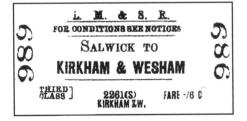

L. M. & S. R.
FOR CONDITIONS SEE NOTICES
SALWICK TO
KIRKHAM & WESHAM
THIRD
CLASS   2261(S)   FARE -/6 C
KIRKHAM ZW.

21. A little further west were the impressive Constable Lane water troughs, pictured here on 22nd July 1960. The four track railway is seen to good effect as 'Royal Scot' 4-6-0 no. 46163 *Civil Service Rifleman* passes over them with the 10.35 Euston – Blackpool Central service. This train would be routed via Lytham and the Coast Line. (P.J.Fitton)

22. Approaching Salwick station on 28th September 1963 is the Immingham shedded Britannia class no. 70039 *Sir Christopher Wren*, with a Blackpool-bound special from Cleethorpes. To the right is the goods yard with loading gauge and two ton hand crane, but time was running out as this only stayed open for another six months, closing on 23rd March 1964. (P.Claxton)

SALWICK

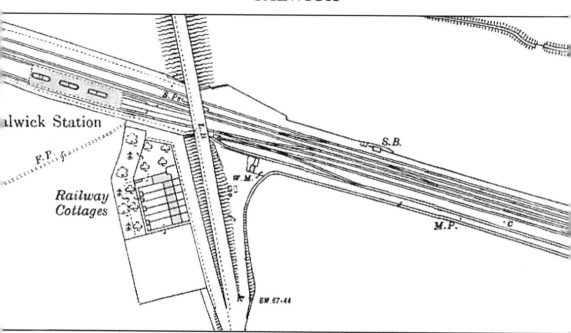

IV. In 1932, similar to Lea Road, Salwick station also had an island platform and both closed in 1938. Salwick itself had a goods siding, and this was extended into the nearby BNFL Springfields Works, when it opened in the late 1940s.

23. The station was opened in 1842 by the PWR and was initially called Salwick Road. After almost 100 years, it closed on 2nd May 1938, only to be reopened on 8th April 1940. It became unstaffed on 18th January 1971. Avoiding the station on 8th August 1964 is Horwich-built Standard 4 no. 76087 with the 10.55 SO Manchester Victoria to Blackpool North service. (P.J.Fitton)

24. On 12th August 1974 a class 124 Trans-Pennine DMU runs past the island platform with the 17.20 Manchester Victoria – Blackpool South train. These attractive Swindon-built units continued in service until 1984. Note the incorrect head code, 1E69, possibly from an earlier run to Leeds, and the wishing well on the overgrown platform. (P.J.Fitton)

25. Less than three years after the previous image, all the station buildings have gone, strangely only leaving the roof. On 25th June 1977, diesel no. 25057 heads an engineers saloon towards Kirkham. After 24 years on the main line the latter was preserved at the North Norfolk Railway. (P.J.Fitton)

26. Considerable freight ran along the Fylde lines well into the 1990s. Nitric acid tanks and ferry vans were taken into the Springfield Works, seen behind, while there was a good volume of chemical traffic to ICI on the former Fleetwood line. On 6th June 1988, no. 47222 *Appleby Frodingham* brings a loaded Stanlow – Burn Naze train past the 1889 vintage signal box. Although still carrying its Salwick No.2 board, the 30-lever box had, in fact, just been simply Salwick from November 1975. The box lights were switched off for the last time on the night of 10th November 2017. (J.Matthews)

EAST OF KIRKHAM

27. Situated between Salwick and Kirkham South Junction were two signal boxes, the first of these being at Spen Lane. The original 18 lever L&YR one, built in 1897, was burnt down and replaced in 1954 by this LMS type that was in use until 28th June 1970. On 18th May 1964, Blackpool's Black 5 no. 44947 heads towards Preston with a local service. The engine was a product of Horwich Works and ironically ended its days just a couple of miles from its birthplace, down the line at Bolton, on 30th June 1968. (P.J.Fitton)

28. Viewed from the 1889 RSC Kirkham South Junction box, in September 1965, is 'Black Five' no. 45421. The extensive track work looks in good shape as the Armstrong Whitworth built 4-6-0 sweeps east with the 10.05 Blackpool South to Euston service. (P.Claxton)

29. The signal box at Treales is pictured here in the early 1970s, by which time the line had been reduced to double track. Built in 1889, this RSC structure was originally equipped with a 20-lever frame, this being replaced at a later date by an L&YR type. The train pictured is a special heading for Blackpool North behind a 1Co-Co1 'Peak'. (P.J.Fitton)

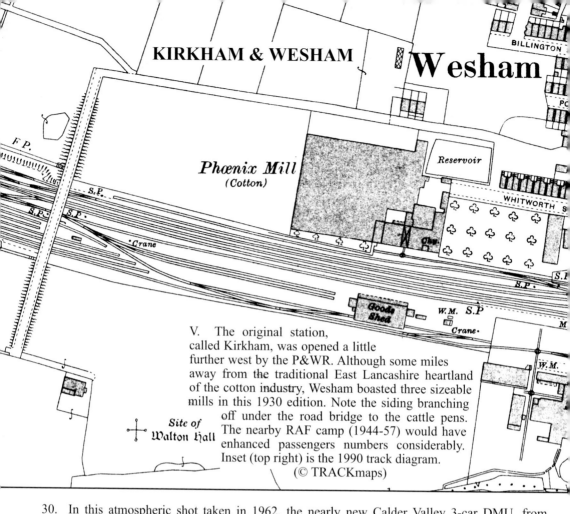

KIRKHAM & WESHAM

Wesham

BILLINGTON

F.P.

S.P.

S.P.

S.P.

Crane

Phœnix Mill
(Cotton)

Reservoir

WHITWORTH S

S.P.

S.P.

Goods Shed

W.M. S.P.

Crane.

W.M.

Site of
Walton Hall

V.   The original station,
called Kirkham, was opened a little
further west by the P&WR. Although some miles
away from the traditional East Lancashire heartland
of the cotton industry, Wesham boasted three sizeable
mills in this 1930 edition. Note the siding branching
off under the road bridge to the cattle pens.
The nearby RAF camp (1944-57) would have
enhanced passengers numbers considerably.
Inset (top right) is the 1990 track diagram.
(© TRACKmaps)

30.   In this atmospheric shot taken in 1962, the nearly new Calder Valley 3-car DMU, from
Bradford to Blackpool Central, has just been relieved of its cargo of mail bags. Worth noting are
the platform surface, water tank and the operational gas lamps. They are Suggs Rochester pattern.
A new footbridge was craned into place on 19th January 2018, as part of the electrification project.
It served a new platform and had lifts. (J.Heydon)

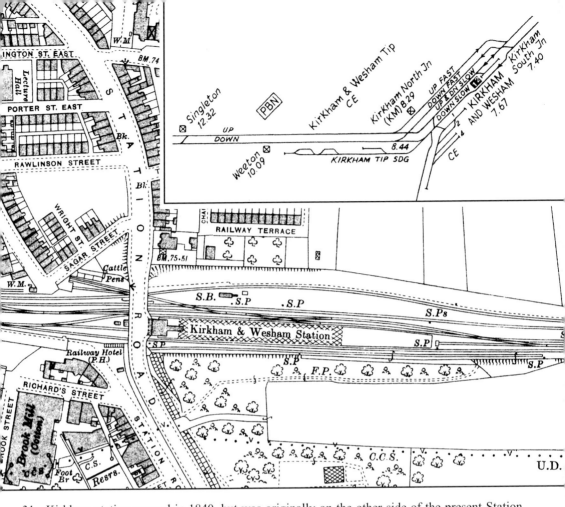

31. Kirkham station opened in 1840, but was originally on the other side of the present Station Road. It was rebuilt on its present site in 1889, and later renamed Kirkham & Wesham. In this well-lit image, diesel loco no. 40140 takes the down fast line with the 17.15 Manchester Victoria – Blackpool North on 3rd September 1975. Two months later, on 16th November, the RSC box would be closed. (P.J.Fitton)

↓ 32. Here is an interesting scene looking back towards the station and Preston. Class B1 no. 61040 *Roedeer* has just 'got the road' for the Marton line, while heading a Knottingley to Blackpool Central excursion on 3rd June 1963. In the distance is an eastbound train, worked by class 5MT 2-6-0 no. 42958. The shunting signal, adjacent to the B1, appears to indicate that the train is going to reverse into the sidings. Another engine waits to take water on the right. (P.J.Fitton)

← 33. Another fascinating view, looking east is from 7th March 1968. Some five months before the total eradication of main line steam, two Stanier-designed engines are at work at Kirkham. Nearest to the camera, short tendered 2-8-0 no. 48423 is shunting vans, while Black Five no. 44816 appears with a load of 20-ton coal wagons from Burnley to Burn Naze. General goods traffic finished here on 25th November of the same year. In the midst of all this activity, a Burlingham Seagull coach is on hand to ferry the permanent-way gang to their next job. Further points of interest are the parachute water tower on the left, Wesham Park Hospital behind it in the distance and, for all MG car fans, an 1100 Mk.1 model, first registered between July and September 1964! (P.J.Fitton)

34. As mentioned earlier, general goods had ended here in late 1968, but the yard was still used for freight, and during 1985 it was employed as a Blue Circle cement depot. On 4th July, passing a morning Euston bound train, is loco no. 37042 on the Saturdays Only Stranraer – Blackpool North service. Leaving at 01.30 in the morning, this train would arrive at Preston at 07.15 before a reversal for the Fylde. Initially numbered D6742, the EE Type 3, was preserved at the Eden Valley Railway after withdrawal in September 2010. (J.Matthews)

35. Now we are at Kirkham North Junction where the three lines to Blackpool diverged. On 19th August 1948 LMS class 5P 4-6-0 no. 10455 has arrived with a pick up goods from Blackpool South, via the Marton line. The Horwich-built engine, which would soon shunt the yard, was built in 1924 and finished its days at Blackpool Central in October 1951 and, by then, was the last of the class. (N.Fields/MLS coll.)

36. Looking in the opposite direction, we see class 8F 2-8-0 no. 48318, with a train of non-corridor coaches, heading west with a special working from Todmorden to Blackpool Central via the Marton line in September 1964. All three Blackpool lines are visible in this view, with the direct up flyover line from Central on the extreme left, the North lines running centrally and the Coast Line to the right. It would appear that the Crewe-built 2-8-0 had been employed to save the need for a banker engine on the climb over Copy Pit. Just visible behind the tender is the 1903 L&YR North Junction box that closed on the night of 10th November 2017. (P.J.Fitton)

37. Here we have moved a little further north as Standard Class 2 no. 84017 brings a train from Fleetwood, under the Marton line flyover and towards North Junction on 14th September 1963. At Kirkham, the two coaches would be attached to a Blackpool Central – Manchester Victoria service. (P.Claxton)

38. A later view of North Junction is from 2nd May 1970. The 11.55 Blackpool South to Euston train was the final service to negotiate the crossover from the Coast Line to the up fast line and is behind diesel no. D441. This loco was numbered 50041 in May 1978 and later carried the name *Bulwark*. (P.J.Fitton)

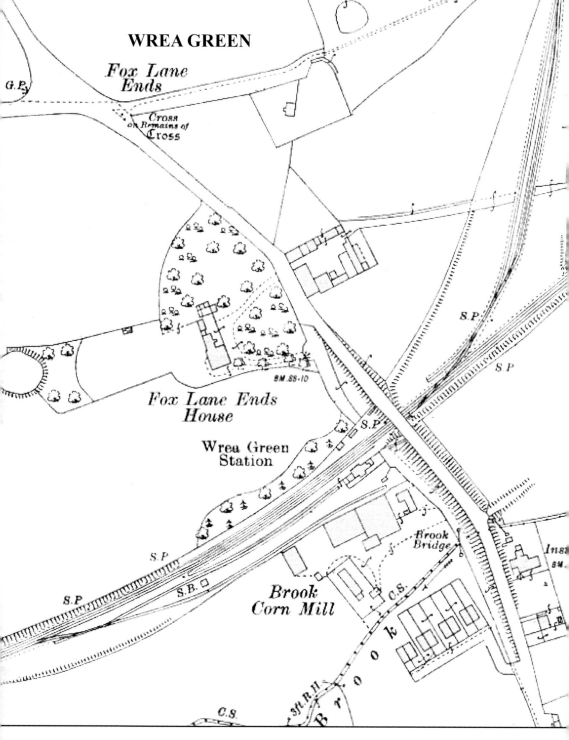

VI. A typical small village station is seen in the early 1930s. In this view we have goods sidings, a signal box and the junction that ran north towards the main Preston to Blackpool lines. Over the years there has been talk of re-opening, but it remained closed in 2018. The name was spelt Wray Green until 1875.

39. We are now travelling along the Coast route, later known as the Blackpool South line. Before Wrea Green there was a four-lever RSC box of 1884 vintage, named Ribby, which lasted until the late 1930s. Heading for Central station, on 6th July 1933, is Horwich-built 0-6-0 LMS no. 12318, that originally carried L&YR no. 1296. (F.Dean)

40. Wrea Green station is pictured around 1900, looking towards Lytham. In the station is an L&YR 2-4-2T with a rake of ex-works Attock bogie coaches. Opened by the PWR in 1846, it closed to passengers on 25th June 1961. Goods trains that visited the sidings behind the train operated until 13th August 1965, and the 1889 16-lever signal box was in use until September 1965. (P.Laming coll.)

41. Shortly before closure, the Station Master checks that all is in order on 24th June 1961. Not stopping today is the 9.15am Blackpool Central - Manchester Victoria train, giving no chance for passengers to see the closure notice on the station house to the left. Blackpool's class 5 4-6-0 no. 45442 is in charge. (P.J.Fitton)

42. We are now looking from the west with this view of Wrea Green on 18th August 1962. The class 5MT 2-6-0 no. 42863, which appears almost ex-works, is heading the SO Castleford to Blackpool Central service. Also of interest is the signalman's car, as well as the goods yard and coal wagon being emptied. (P.J.Fitton)

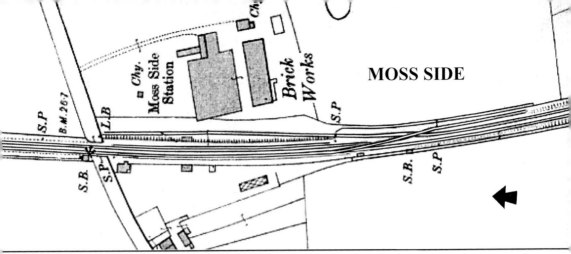

MOSS SIDE

VII. With the large Brown Moss Side to the west, the station's name was probably easy to decide on. Again a very rural scene here in 1909, but we do have a brick works by the railway. Moss Side closed for goods in August 1955, some six years before the passenger trains stopped calling.

43.   On the final day of passenger services, 25th June 1961, we have a poignant view of a typical country stop. The same Station Master as Wrea Green, seen on the extreme right, oversees the arrival of the 4.50pm Sundays Preston to Blackpool Central train, headed by Standard Class 2 2-6-2T no. 84010. With the help of Lancashire County Council, the halt was re-opened in November 1983. (P.J.Fitton)

44. There had been two signal boxes here, one next to the goods sidings dating from 1893, and the one pictured here on 4th July 1966. Although the station was closed, the box is still guarding the road crossing as class 4 2-6-4T no. 42096 heads the 09.05 Euston – Blackpool South working. At the time, a Lostock Hall resident, the engine has received some front end paintwork, although the chimney top is broken. Moss Side Station box survived until 1983, while the loco was disposed of in May 1967. (P.J.Fitton)

EAST OF LYTHAM

45. 1¼ miles before stopping at Lytham, one passes over the site of Warton Junction, which carried trains on the half-mile branch to Lytham Dock. It was open from 1846 into the 1930s. Through a typical Fylde landscape and heading towards Lytham, we catch a glimpse of Sulzer Type 4 'Peak' no. D58. The train is the 09.30 Sundays Only Manchester Victoria to Blackpool Central service. The original box at Warton was destroyed in an accident in 1924, and this LMS replacement continued in its place until closure in October 1963, around six months after this photo. The diesel loco was re-numbered 45043 on 31st December 1973, when it received the name *The King's Own Royal Border Regiment*. (P.J.Fitton)

46. Before reaching Lytham there was Lytham Goods signal box, built in 1895. The goods yard closed on 1st April 1963. On 5th July 1966, class 4P 2-6-4T no. 42187 passes with the 09.05 Euston to Blackpool South train, which it had worked from Preston. The box was in operation until 4th February 1967, just six weeks before the engine was withdrawn from Lostock Hall. (P.J.Fitton)

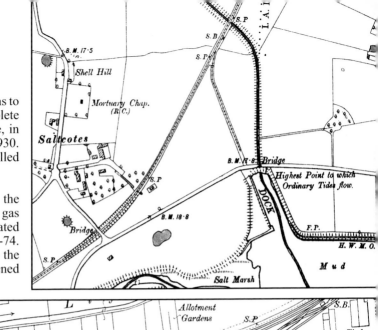

➔ VIIIa. The 1894 survey at 4ins to 1 mile shows parts of the incomplete Lytham Dock line. It was in use, in part, between 1846 and about 1930. It had a passenger station called WARTON in 1865-74.

VIIIb. The 1911 survey shows the extent of the goods yard and gas works. This area had accommodated the terminal station from 1846-74. The line to the left border and to the station in the bottom map opened in 1874.

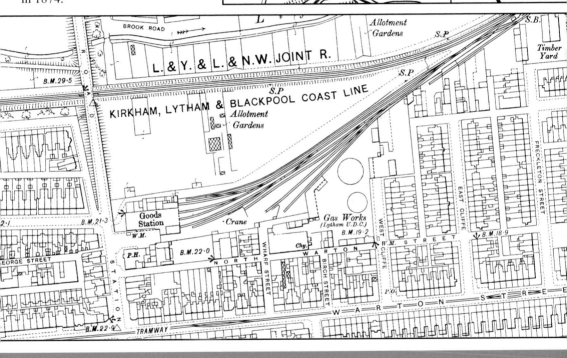

LYTHAM

VIIIc. The station has been in use since 1863. The road over the bridge runs directly south to the pier.

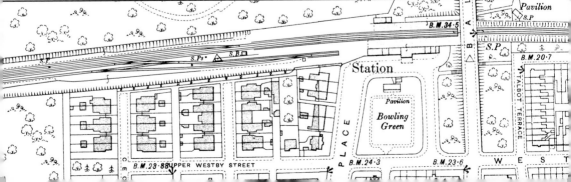

47. Departing for Blackpool in the 1920s is a class 2P 2-4-2T loco with its collection of L&YR Attock coaches. Lytham Station signal box was an L&YR type that survived until 12th October 1971. On the right is the bay platform once used by the Blackpool to Lytham rail motor service. (LOSA)

48. A much later view is seen on 19th April 1968. Steam is nearing the end, but still a regular performer was Derby built no. 44816, seen with the 12.44 from Preston and devoid of its smokebox number. Worth noting on the far platform are the L&YR bench and trolleys. (P.J.Fitton)

ANSDELL & FAIRHAVEN

49. Passing under Ansdell footbridge on 3rd March 1962 are a Bradford – Blackpool Central DMU and class 4 4-6-0 no. 75046 with the 11.45 Blackpool Central to Manchester Victoria service. By 2018, the much reduced Ansdell station had an hourly service from Blackpool South to Preston and East Lancashire. (P.Claxton)

50. With a train for Preston on the wintry morning of 28th December 1962, we catch a view of class 5 4-6-0 no. 45442. The loco was built by Armstrong Whitworth in 1937 and spent time at Patricroft shed before finishing its days at Kingmoor in late 1966. The goods depot to the left was still open. The yard closed on 24th April 1967. (P.J.Fitton)

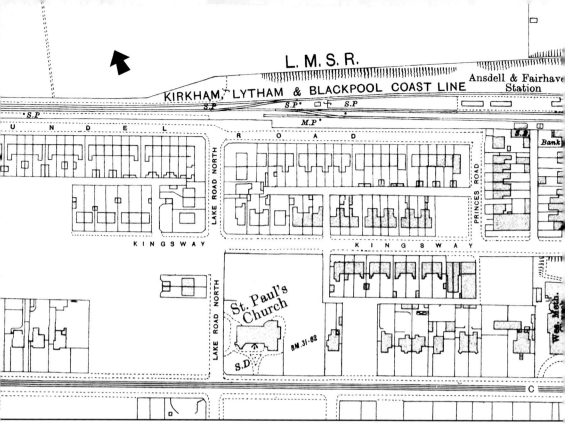

51. In this idyllic picture, taken on 13th August 1965, class 8F 2-8-0 no. 48199 has arrived with the final coal train, whose loaded wagons it has reversed into the siding, for the waiting road lorries. The yard was equipped with a 5-ton crane and, in its heyday, would handle a variety of general goods. (P.J.Fitton)

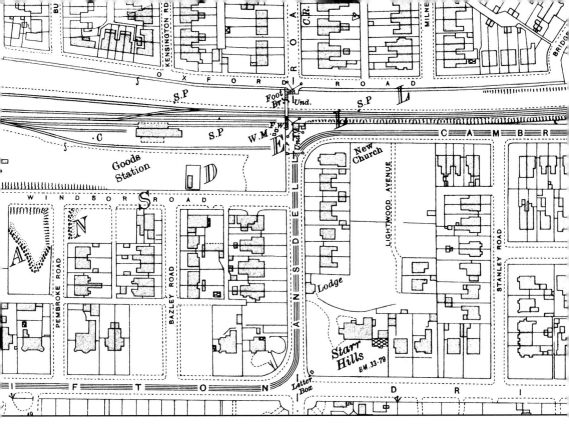

IX. The first station opened here in 1872 and was called Ansdell, but by 1906 it had moved some 300m due west and been renamed Ansdell & Fairhaven. Situated close to the Royal Lytham and St. Annes Golf Club, the station handles many thousands of passengers during the Open Golf Championship. The slight down side is that 'The Open' is only held at the course every six or seven years, and the single line railway is totally inadequate for handling the number of trains required for the golf fans.

52. Pictured at the station, on the evening of 14th July 1960, is the 6.0pm SX train from Southport to Blackpool Central. These class 2P 4-4-0s were a rare sight on the Fylde lines and no. 40588, built in 1928, had just over three months left in service. (P.J.Fitton)

53. Demolition is literally in full swing on 10th May 1972, as a local unit for Blackpool South passes. The buildings and roof are being reduced to a pile of bricks and rubble by men working on the roof top with no safety equipment, over two years before the introduction of the Health & Safety Act in 1974. The 1903 L&YR box had already closed on 12th October 1971. (P.J.Fitton)

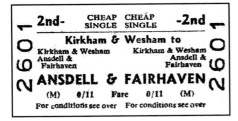

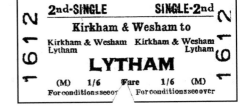

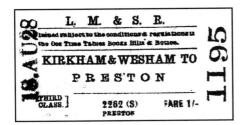

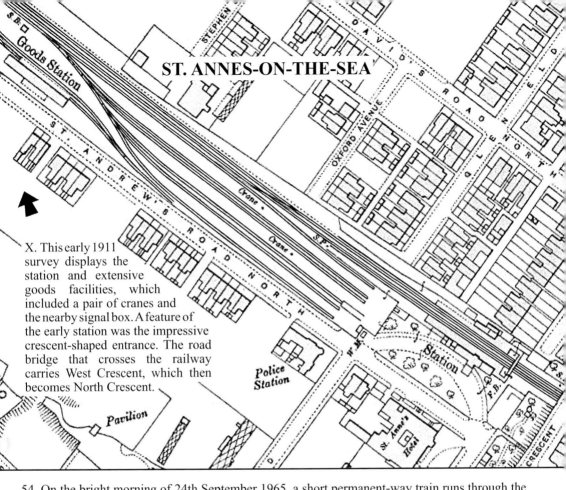

ST. ANNES-ON-THE-SEA

X. This early 1911 survey displays the station and extensive goods facilities, which included a pair of cranes and the nearby signal box. A feature of the early station was the impressive crescent-shaped entrance. The road bridge that crosses the railway carries West Crescent, which then becomes North Crescent.

54. On the bright morning of 24th September 1965, a short permanent-way train runs through the station for Preston. At the head is Standard Class 5 no. 73132, built at Derby in September 1956 and one of 172 class members. This particular loco was fitted with Caprotti valve gear and had a very short life that ended at Patricroft in March 1965. (P.J.Fitton)

55. The first station at St. Annes-on-the-Sea was opened by the Blackpool & Lytham Railway in 1863 and called Cross Slack. Re-located in November 1875, it received its present grand title a little over a year later. Now, just a single line survives, but on 15th August 1961 this was far from the case, as 1926-built Fowler Jinty 0-6-0T no. 47319 is caught shunting a local engineers train. (P.J.Fitton)

56. There was a substantial goods yard and depot pictured in this scene on 24th June 1963. The imposing goods shed stands proudly looking over operations, which included the coal yard to the right. General freight and livestock were both handled, with the help of a 5-ton crane, but closure still came on 25th November 1968. (P.J.Fitton)

57. This grand panorama is looking back towards the station on 7th March 1964. Jubilee class no. 45574 *India* is making a spirited departure with a Blackpool Central bound service. This well-known Blackpool engine, of 1934 vintage, was finally withdrawn from Leeds Holbeck in March 1966. The signal box remained in operation until around 1983. (P.Claxton)

58. Most of the station buildings and the footbridge were still in situ on 7th May 1983. Things were soon to change, as the line was singled and virtually everything in view was demolished. On the right is the 07.43 Kirkham to Blackpool South train in the company of the 07.50 Blackpool South – Preston DMU. (J.Matthews)

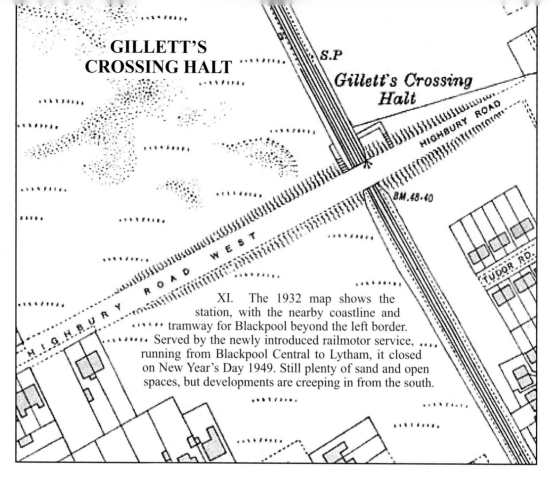

GILLETT'S CROSSING HALT

Gillett's Crossing Halt

S.P

HIGHBURY ROAD

BM. 48·40

HIGHBURY ROAD WEST

TUDOR RD.

XI. The 1932 map shows the station, with the nearby coastline and tramway for Blackpool beyond the left border. Served by the newly introduced railmotor service, running from Blackpool Central to Lytham, it closed on New Year's Day 1949. Still plenty of sand and open spaces, but developments are creeping in from the south.

59. This small halt was opened on 1st October 1913 and closed briefly in World War I, but permanently on 11th September 1939. Pictured around 1928, Hughes Baltic no. 11117 heads towards St. Annes with a train from Blackpool. Built at Horwich in 1924, it was retired from Lostock Hall in July 1941. (E.Ashworth)

60. Looking east, possibly on the same day as the previous image, the prototype 500hp Beardmore diesel electric train has just passed the Halt on a Lytham to Blackpool Central working. The Old Links Golf Club, founded in 1901, is clearly seen on the left. The 6941yd par 72 course has been the venue for many top tournaments, and was to host the 2018 Open Final Qualifying. (E.Ashworth)

61. Passing the Old Links Golf Club and heading towards St. Annes in 1956 is the aptly named *Lytham St Annes*, 'Patriot' class 4-6-0 no. 45548. The name would be used again when carried later by Peak diesel loco no. D60, later no. 45022. (E.Woods)

SQUIRES GATE

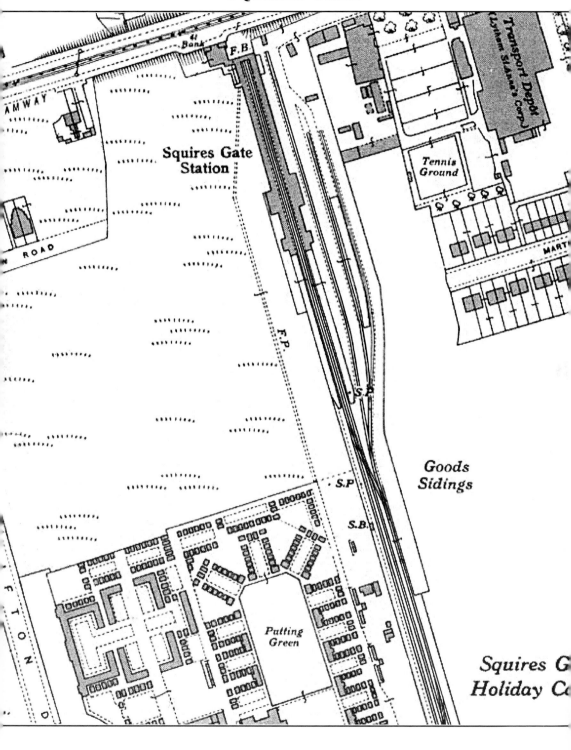

← XII. In this early 1940s record we see the station, goods sidings and holiday camp, later known as Pontins, which survived until 2009, Hi-de-Hi.

62. In this photo, circa 1935, we look south at the station, with its LMS notice boards. A nearby station had opened in April 1865 called Stoney Hill, but was only open seven years. The one seen opened in September 1931 and still survives, but in a much reduced state. The nearby airport attracted some passengers to the station, but the last scheduled flights to Dublin and the Isle of Man operated in November 2014. In the distance to the left, is the goods yard that closed on 2nd November 1964, while on the right is the L&YR signal box, which operated until March 1965. (LOSA)

L.Y. & L.N.W. JOINT RLYS.
Issued subject to the regulations and conditions of the Co's Time Tables, Books, Bills & Notices. Available on day of issue only.
THIRD CLASS
ANSDELL
TO
LYTHAM
266 Lytham   Fare 1d.

L. M. & S. R.
FOR CONDITIONS SEE NOTICES
LYTHAM TO
SQUIRES GATE
THIRD CLASS   22•5(S)   FARE -/9 C
S   S GATE

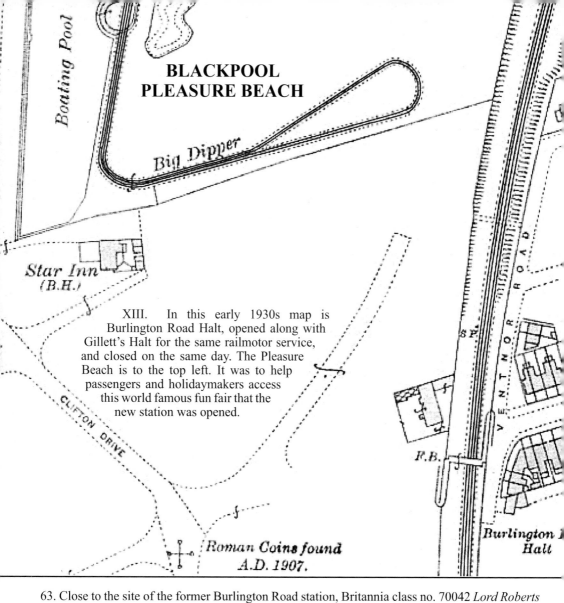

BLACKPOOL
PLEASURE BEACH

Boating Pool

Big Dipper

Star Inn
(B.H.)

XIII.   In this early 1930s map is Burlington Road Halt, opened along with Gillett's Halt for the same railmotor service, and closed on the same day. The Pleasure Beach is to the top left. It was to help passengers and holidaymakers access this world famous fun fair that the new station was opened.

CLIFTON DRIVE

VENTNOR ROAD

S.P.

P.B.

Roman Coins found
A.D. 1907.

Burlington
Halt

63. Close to the site of the former Burlington Road station, Britannia class no. 70042 *Lord Roberts* runs south on 24th July 1961, in charge of the 17.05 Blackpool South – Euston working. These 4-6-2 locos first appeared in 1951, and a total of 55 were built, many with great names in British history. (P.Claxton)

64. Passing the Pleasure Beach on 11th July 1975, we have Sulzer-powered diesel no. 25202 heading a weed killer special. The loco was numbered D7552 when it left Derby Works in June 1965. The Amusement Park, visible behind the train, was opened in 1896 and had a peak number of 5.5m fun seekers in 2007. (P.J.Fitton)

65. Burlington Road Halt opened in 1919, but was closed on 11th September 1939. Blackpool Pleasure Beach was eventually built, and here we see a three-car DMU from Preston to Blackpool South calling on the day of opening, 13th April 1987. (J.Matthews)

← XIV. South Shore station opened in 1863 and is shown as Lytham Road, on this 1911 map. Further north is Waterloo Road station, which opened in 1903 to coincide with the arrival of the Marton fast line from Kirkham. Lytham Road closed on 14th July 1916, after Waterloo Road became the main station at the junction. From March 1932 it was called Blackpool South and was then provided with four platforms.

66. On opening in 1863 this was the only intermediate station on the Blackpool & Lytham Railway. In this scene from around 1907, the grand station and its buildings look in good condition with Blackpool Tower just visible, left. Interestingly, one of the station buildings was later moved to become a local residence. (LOSA)

BLACKPOOL SOUTH

67. This northward panorama features the roofing over all four platforms and the roof of the main building is on the left. In 1958, class 5 4-6-0 no. 45415 is ready to move off with an afternoon Coast Line service. The goods yard closed on 14th August 1967. (E.Johnson)

68. Arriving at South station around 1960 is a train on the direct Marton line. The light is just right as 'Jubilee' class 4-6-0 no. 45684 *Jutland* passes the L&YR signals and heads for Central. There were 191 of these LMS engines built in the mid-1930s; many named after faraway places with strange sounding names. (E.Johnson)

69. On 3rd May 1970, the last day of main line trains at Blackpool South, Brush Type 4 no. D1850 is pictured with the 10.15 departure to London Euston. The abandoned former Marton Line platforms are looking very much the worse for wear on the right. The diesel, built at Crewe in 1965, was re-numbered 47200 on 31st December 1973, and carried three different names, *Jackdaw*, *Herbert Austin* and *The Fosse Way*. (P.J.Fitton)

70. In this very forlorn scene, we catch a view of the final Blackpool South to Manchester Victoria service. On 14th May 1982, the driver glances at his newspaper whilst waiting to set off with the 07.48 departure. The main station buildings are still intact, but nature appears to be moving in. (J.Matthews)

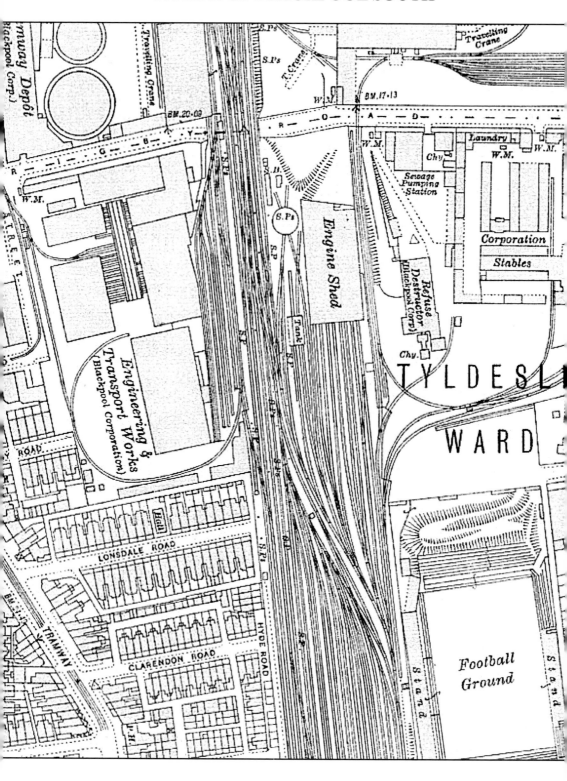

← XV. A 1932 extract of the massive expanse of sidings between Blackpool's South and Central stations can be seen. Lines appear to run in all directions, to the Corporation Works on the left, the Central MPD in the middle and stables to the right. The famous 'Tangerines' Football Ground on Bloomfield Road is at the bottom of the map and, if you found the right seat, you could watch the footballers and railway both hard at work.

71. A little further north were the extensive carriage sidings at Bloomfield Road, part of which can be seen here on 5th July 1964. 'Britannia' class 4-6-2 no. 70005 *John Milton* makes a fine sight, as it heads south with a return special to Cannock running via the Coast Line. To the right is Blackpool F.C.'s ground, proudly displaying an advert for C&S 'XL' Ales. The local brewery, with the full name of Catterall & Swarbrick, was based in Talbot Road but ceased trading in 1974. Just visible on the left is Bloomfield Road box; when built by the L&YR in 1902 it featured a 40-lever frame, but it closed on 1st November 1964. (P.J.Fitton)

2nd · SINGLE	SINGLE · 2nd
St. Annes-on-Sea To	
St. Annes-on-Sea	St. Annes-on-Sea
Blackpool (South)	Blackpool (South)
BLACKPOOL	
(SOUTH)	
(M) 1/2	Fare 1/2 (M)
For conditions see over	For conditions see over

2nd-SINGLE	SINGLE-2nd
Ansdell & Fairhaven to	
Ansdell & Fairhaven	Ansdell & Fairhaven
Blackpool (South)	Blackpool (South)
BLACKPOOL (SOUTH)	
(M)	Fare (M)
For conditions see over	For conditions see over

BLACKPOOL CENTRAL

XVI. Blackpool Central station is shown in 1932, some 21 years after it was noted as the world's busiest railway station. The six covered platforms and the eight for excursion traffic can be clearly picked out. The station closed in early November 1964 amid political wrangling, after the Beeching Plan had recommended keeping Central open and closing Blackpool North! The station, as the name suggests, was very well-situated and convenient for passengers. The beach was close to the left border.

Engine Shed

72. Outside the shed or motive power depot, an interesting array of locos enjoys the summer sunshine of 30th June 1963. From the left are the following, a Jubilee, a 2-6-4T, a 'Royal Scot', a Peak, another 'Royal Scot' no. 46166 *London Rifle Brigade*, 'Black Five' no. 45236 and a Class 40 diesel. (P.J.Fitton)

73. Another view of the depot is shown, this time in 1964. Blackpool Tower again looks over the picture, which shows class 5F 2-6-0 no. 42715 resting between turns. The former LMS engine had arrived on a Saturday Only service from Sheffield, and would stay in service until February 1966. (P.J.Fitton)

↓ 74. This view is inside Blackpool Central shed on 30th May 1964. From the left, the line up is 'Britannia' no. 70007 *Coeur-de-Lion*, 4-6-0 engines nos 45318, 45705 *Seahorse*, 44950 and a Yorkshire Engine Company diesel shunter. (P.J.Fitton)

Central Station

75. This busy scene at the front of the station is from a postcard dating from the 1890s. Opened on 6th April 1863 by the BLRly, it was known as Hounds Hill, before becoming Blackpool Central in 1878, and then extended to 14 platforms during a complete rebuild in 1901. (P.Laming coll.)

76. Words cannot really describe this view of the Excursion Platforms in August 1916. After a day by the seaside, thousands of passengers wait for their trains home to many parts of the country. (LCC Archives)

77. An excellent view of the station, and especially the splendid roof and cross supports is from the 1st July 1951. Former L&YR Hughes loco no. 50455, previously seen at Kirkham, is waiting to leave with a special for York, this being the engine's final run before withdrawal in October. (R.F.Roberts/SLS)

78. Blackpool shedded 'Jubilee' class no. 45574 *India* waits with the 10.15 departure for Manchester Victoria on 30th July 1964. As this was its final working to Manchester, after doing so since 1937, the photographer had cleaned the engine especially. (P.J.Fitton)

79. With the train's head code chalked on the smokebox front, class 5 no. 45078 makes a spirited departure with the 16.00 to Manchester Exchange. The date is 29th August 1964 and the 4-6-0 had just over a year to run before withdrawal from Crewe South. (P.J.Fitton)

80. After the closure of Central on 2nd November 1964, the nearby 1901 L&YR Spen Dyke box lasted a little longer, until July 1965. The signalman peers out as class 5 no. 44905 is turned on the electric turntable on 2nd April 1965. The engine, built at Crewe in October 1945, is being prepared to work the 17.20 Blackpool South to Euston train. (P.J.Fitton)

2. Kirkham Junction to Blackpool North

KIRKHAM JUNCTION

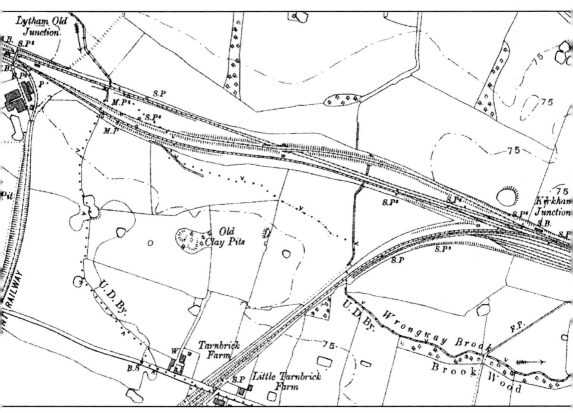

XVII. The main Preston to Blackpool and Fleetwood route crosses this 1909 survey, while separate lines run down towards Wrea Green from Kirkham North Junction and Lytham Old Junction. The flyover for the Marton fast line crosses over the main line, near the centre of the map.

81. Closed in 1967, the main feature of the Marton line was the flyover at Kirkham that allowed up trains easy access to the up fast line. Many of the B1 class were named after gazelles and deer. Here we see no. 61001 *Eland* working the 16.00 SO Blackpool Central to Lincoln service on 10th September 1960, some three years before being retired at Doncaster. (P.J.Fitton)

82. The Marton Line to Blackpool South and Central had closed in 1967, but the flyover was not completely removed for a number of years. We see EE Type 4 no. 40009 with a Leeds – Blackpool North train on the misty morning of 26th July 1980. (J.Matthews)

83. In this rare photograph, dated circa 1930, there is a good view at Lytham Old Junction, later known as Bradkirk. The single line, branching off to the right, was built in 1846 to link Wrea Green and Lytham with the main PWR line to Fleetwood. LMS loco nos 12155 and 12175 double-head a train from Todmorden to Central via the Marton line.
Both these L&YR 0-6-0s were built as early as 1892 with no. 12175 clocking up an incredible 65 years, when withdrawn from Speke Junction. (F.Dean)

84. In this classic view of Bradkirk on 3rd September 1960, 'Black Five' no. 44949 heads a Manchester-bound empty stock train routed around the Kirkham Flyover onto the slow line. Introduced as LMS no. 4949 in February 1946, it ran until June 1968, around a year before the closure of the 1903 L&YR box. (P.J.Fitton)

SINGLETON

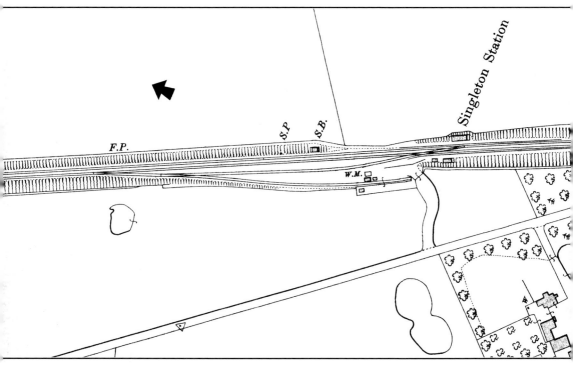

F.P.   S.P.   S.B.   W.M.   Singleton Station

XVIII. Heading towards Blackpool North there was a station at Weeton until 1843, but little evidence of this could be uncovered. Therefore, the next station was Singleton with very little to note, other than the signal box, loop line and siding. This is the 1911 edition.

85. This small rural station was opened by the P&WR in 1872. Close by was Singleton Park estate, built in 1874 by T.H. Miller, who, for a period, owned the vast Horrockses cotton factories in Preston. Pictured in 1897, the station master appears to be on the extreme left with one of his children. The station was closed on 2nd May 1932, but goods were handled until September 1939. (M.Chew)

86. Trains pass at Singleton Station signal box on 30th July 1983. An early L&YR box built in 1879 with 16 levers, it saw a life of just over 100 years and by this time had a distinct lean. As a local DMU heads off towards Preston, Peak class no. 45007 passes with the 08.00 SO York to Blackpool North working. The Class 45s, with their Sulzer power units, were capable of 90mph and this particular member ran from 1961 until July 1988. (J.Matthews)

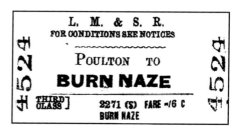

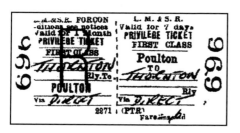

POULTON-LE-FYLDE

Labels on map:

B.M.41·4

Poulton View Farm

Pool Lodge

S.P

S.B.

C.S.

C.S.

S.Ps

L. & Y. & L. & N.W. JOINT R.
PRESTON & WYRE LINE

Def: v.

Watercourse

Horse Bridge

C.S.

C.C.S.

Poulton Curve Halt
S.P
B.M. 40·3

S.P

S.P

C.S.
U.D. Bdy.

S.P

L. BARN STREET

LONGFIELD AVENUE

LONGFIELD PLACE

S.P.

S.P

F.P.
Springfield House

Congregational Church
Sunday School

F.P.

Auction Mart

S.Ps

XIX. The complex lines at Poulton-le-Fylde are shown here in 1912 at 15ins to 1 mile. The first station, on the P&WR to Fleetwood, opened at 'The Breck' (top right) in 1840. This was followed, in 1846, with the arrival of the branch line from Blackpool providing a triangle at the original Poulton. In 1893, a fatal accident at its sharp curve to Preston led to the new south curve and station being opened in 1896, both still in use today. To the north, a new curve was built in 1899 to allow trains to run between Blackpool and Fleetwood, and a halt on the curve was open from 1909 until closure in 1952.

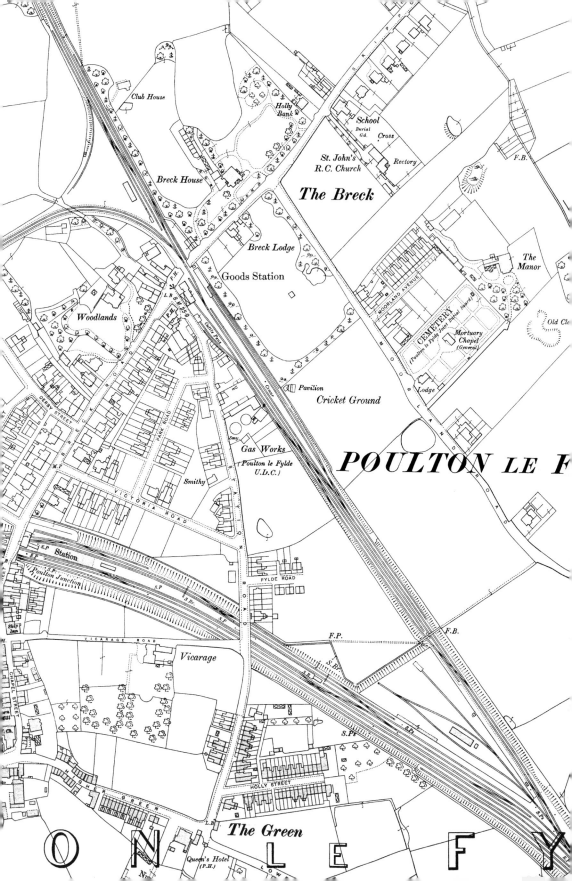

Club House

Holly Bank

Breck House

School
Burial Gd.
Cross

St. John's
R.C. Church

Rectory

F.B.

The Breck

Breck Lodge

Goods Station

The Manor

Woodlands

MOORLAND AVENUE

CEMETERY
(Poulton le Fylde Joint Burial Board)

Mortuary
Chapel
(General)

Old Cl

DERBY STREET

PARK ROAD

Smithy

Pavilion

Cricket Ground

Lodge

M.P.

VICTORIA ROAD

Gas Works
Poulton le Fylde
U.D.C.

POULTON LE F

MOORLAND ROAD

Station

S.P.

Poulton Junction

S.P.

S.P.

FYLDE ROAD

Ship
Inn

VICARAGE ROAD

Vicarage

F.P.

F.B.

S.Br.

S.P.

CHAPEL STREET

Ch.

HOLLY STREET

HIGHER GREEN

S.P.

S.P.

S.Br.

O N L E F Y

The Green

Queen's Hotel
(P.H.)

South of the Station

87. Seen three months before the end of steam, class 8F no. 48730 appears to be in good order. It is pictured in charge of an up freight train from the Fleetwood branch, with Poulton No.2 box in the distance, which closed on 18th July 1971. (T.Heavyside)

Box No. 1

88. An interesting glimpse of the former track bed of the original P&WR line to Fleetwood, as it is seen heading off to 'The Breck' in the top right corner. Open between 1840 and 1896 as the route to Fleetwood, it was then used for goods traffic for Poulton until 1968. The No. 1 signal box was an L&YR design from 1896, and lasted just two and a half years after this picture was taken on 12th July 1975. The EE diesel loco no. 50040, which is bringing a Euston train south, was new in September 1968 and named *Leviathan* 10 years later. (T.Heavyside)

The Halt

89. This is a rare view of Poulton Curve Halt, which can be found on the west of the triangle, on the map. Class 2P 2-4-2T no. 10750 is waiting to leave on 30th April 1948. The halt was in use from 1st February 1909 to 1st December 1952. (SLS)

The Station

90. An early scene at Poulton, probably around 1910, where we see an L&YR 'Highflyer' at the head of a southbound train. The track to the right later became a car park, but the near line remains. This fine looking engine was built at Horwich in 1901 and featured 7ft 3in driving wheels. (J.M.Tomlinson/P.Laming coll.)

91. This postcard view is from about 1920 and includes Breck Road, granite setts and a then rare example of internal combustion. The station was built on the bridge and was still in use almost 100 years later, largely unchanged. (P.Laming coll.)

92. One of five signal boxes at Poulton, No. 2 box was situated at the south end of the platforms and was opened in 1896 with 46 levers. In 1928, an 0-6-0 loco, carrying the LMS no. 4474, heads south out of the station with the signalman checking the road ahead. (I.Robinson coll.)

93. Seen veering off to the right is the line to Burn Naze and Fleetwood. On 9th September 1984, no. 40143 arrives on the 13.55 Blackpool North to Manchester Victoria train, passing a Swindon DMU, which includes a class 101 coach in the middle. The large No. 3 signal box is of L&YR design and, when opened in 1896, had 74 levers. It had a long life but closed for the final time in the early hours of 11th November 2017. (P.J.Fitton)

Carleton Crossing

94. After leaving Poulton-le-Fylde, as we approach Layton, there was this splendid signal box guarding the level crossing at Carleton. This box was the third at this location, being built by the LMS in 1924. On 11th May 1963, 'Peak' no. D73 is hurrying over Carleton Crossing, bound for Blackpool North with the 16.03 from Manchester Victoria. (P.J.Fitton)

LAYTON

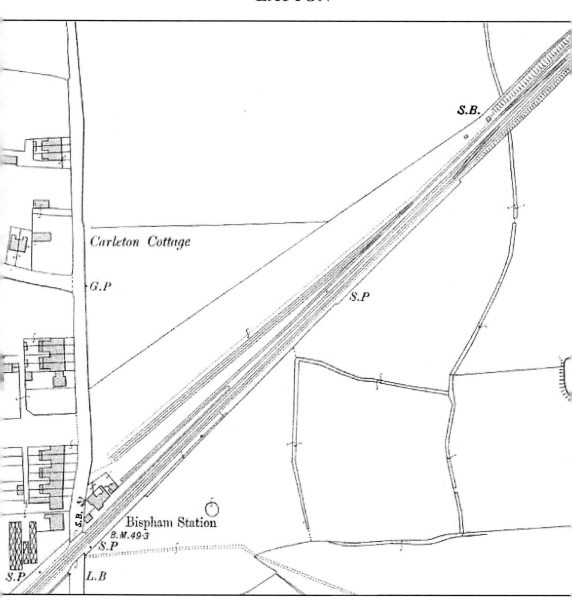

Carleton Cottage

G.P

S.B.

S.P

S.B.

Bispham Station

B.M.49·3

S.P

S.P   *L.B*

XX. The present station opened in May 1867 and replaced an earlier one beyond the lower border. On opening it was called Bispham, this being changed to Layton on 4th July 1938. This map from 1912 shows the original station, two signal boxes, one close to the station building and the other, a little nearer Poulton, overseeing the sidings.

95. Passing on 15th September 1962, ex-LMS class 5F no. 42748 is seen on a Hadfield – Blackpool special running under the art deco style concrete road bridge. It was replaced during the electrification closure. The 2-6-0 was new from Crewe Works in 1927 and enjoyed a long 37-year career, before withdrawal from Gorton. (P.J.Fitton)

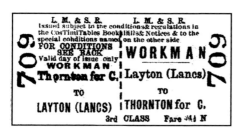

XXI. Before arrival at Blackpool North was No. 1 signal box at the entrance to the extensive carriage sidings. The original box from 1893 was replaced by the BR type in the 1950s. This 1912 extract includes the engine shed and the abattoir's short siding, top right.

96. The loco shed was situated at the station end of the carriage sidings. Here, sitting outside the depot on the bright spring morning of 4th April 1949 is ex-L&YR LMS no. 10889. This 2-4-2T was built at Horwich in 1910 and withdrawn a few miles away at Central shed only six months after this picture was taken. (H.C.Casserley)

97. We are now inside the motive power depot itself on 18th April 1965. Here, we have a train-spotter's delight, as we see from left to right, a Sulzer Type 2 no. D5190, the nose of a 'Peak', Class 40 no. D299, 'Jubilee' class no. 45643 *Rodney* and, finally, Brush no. D5856, later a class 31. The shed had initially closed in early 1964, but re-opened in November that year for servicing only, after Central shed had closed. (P.J.Fitton)

98. Pictured near the shed turntable on 29th August 1965 is a pair of locos that have been turned. On the right we see 'Jubilee' 4-6-0 no. 45563 *Australia* and an unidentified Black Five on the left. Just visible in the distance is a split head coded Peak. (P.J.Fitton)

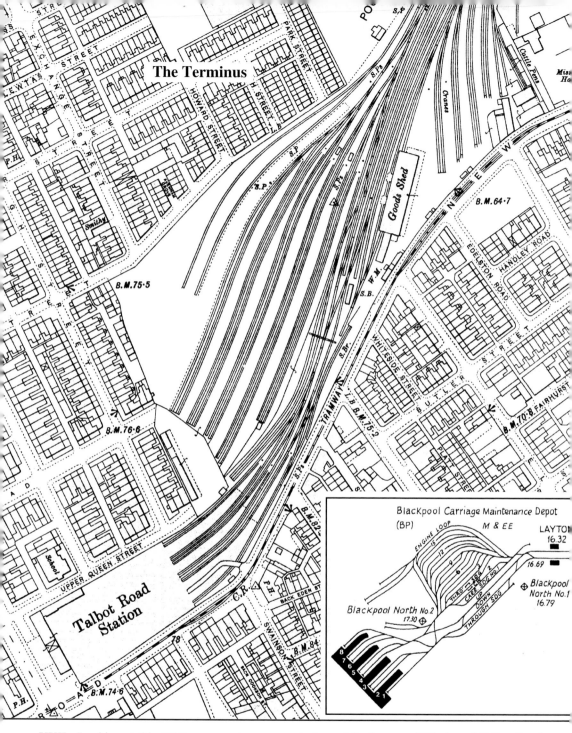

XXII. Looking at this 1912 map, we have a great view of the layout of Blackpool Talbot Road station. After electrification and remodelling, the new Blackpool North would be reduced to just six platforms. Surrounded by rows and rows of dwellings we note the tramway snaking across the map. At the top are the goods shed and sidings that, until the early 1980s, housed the Co-op coal depot. The street tramway here closed in 1963, leaving Blackpool with only a waterfront route. Inset is the 1990 layout. (© TRACKmaps)

99. The first station opened in April 1846 and was simply known as Blackpool. It became Talbot Road in 1872 and its first rebuild followed in 1898. The rebuilt station consisted of platform nos 1 to 6 covered by two parallel train sheds, with open platforms nos 7 to 16 used mainly in the busy summer months. The final name change, to Blackpool North, came on 17th March 1932. This image, from around 1900, shows a 4-4-2 L&YR loco posing with its train crew. (P.Laming coll.)

100. In pre-grouping days, Talbot Road was a joint L&YR and LNWR station. On 2nd August, probably 1916, the impressive excursion platform departure board directs passengers to various places, including Doncaster Grand Central, Sheffield Midland and Birmingham. On the left can be seen two LNWR engines. The large board also promotes the virtues of Brands A1 steak sauce, first produced in 1831 and amazingly still available from your high street today!
(Lancashire C.C. Archives)

101. This panorama of North station was taken from No. 2 signal box on Whit Monday 1966. The 79tons 11cwt 4-6-0 'Jubilee' class no. 45565 *Victoria* departs on a return special to Bradford, with a number of Black Fives waiting their turn. On the far left, just discernible through the smoke, is the L&YR No. 3 signal box. It was built by the L&YR and opened in 1896 with 100 levers. It was first known as Talbot Road No. 3. (P.Claxton)

102. The station frontage was most impressive and, on 13th July 1967, the grand building looks in excellent order, with its large clock. Even the entrance gate posts have style. Two large signs point the way to the 16 platforms, as a Rail Freight parcels van sets off with its next delivery. (H.C.Casserley)

103. With one year of steam to go, no. 45000 is seen about to depart with the 09.35 SX service to Windermere on 21st August 1967. Originally LMS no. 5000, it was built in March 1935 and ended its days on the main line at Lostock Hall in October 1967. The story had a happy ending for the 4-6-0, as it was preserved and sent to the National Railway Museum at York. (P.J.Fitton)

104. An impressive telephoto shot here for all diesel, as well as signalling, fans. The Tower stands tall on 29th May 1972 with a great line up of returning specials, waiting in the early evening light. From the left we can see nos D6718, D1960, D263 and D1100, proving that you don't necessarily need a steam engine to make a classic image. (P.J.Fitton)

105. Dawn is just breaking over the station on 11th December 1982 and a great sight was here for 'Whistler' fans. On the left, no. 40044 waits with a 'Mystery Excursion' special, accompanied by no. 40027 with the 'Fylde Flyer' rail tour for York. Both locos had been built at the English Electric Vulcan Foundry in late 1959. (J.Matthews)

106. A fitting finale to this section is this view of no. 37407 *Blackpool Tower* leaving with the 10.15 SO train to Holyhead on 8th July 1995. Passing the 120-lever No. 2 signal box, built in 1896, the EE type 3 diesel was first numbered D6605, and carried the name *Loch Long* for over eight years, until January 1995. The box was there right to the very end, which came in the early hours of 11th November 2017, as the railway closed to prepare for its new life under electrification. (P.J.Fitton)

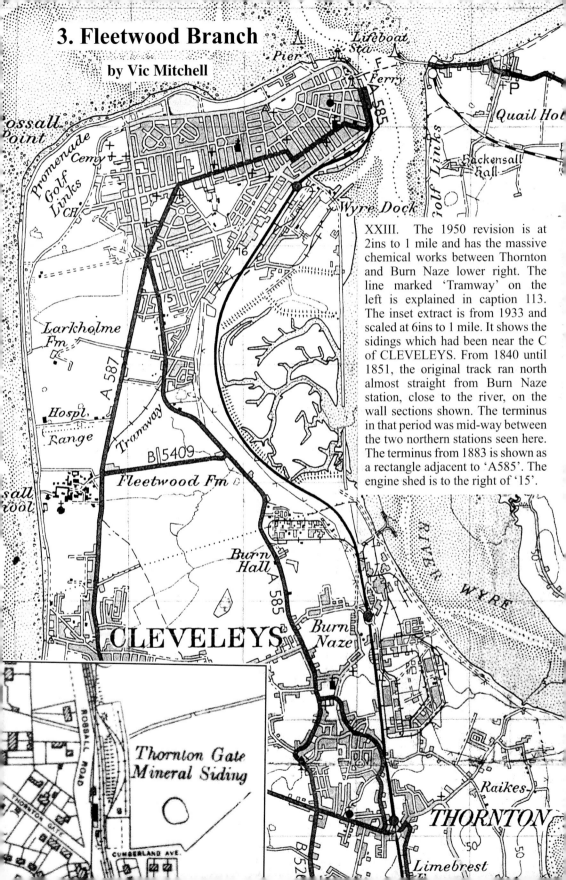

3. Fleetwood Branch

by Vic Mitchell

XXIII. The 1950 revision is at 2ins to 1 mile and has the massive chemical works between Thornton and Burn Naze lower right. The line marked 'Tramway' on the left is explained in caption 113. The inset extract is from 1933 and scaled at 6ins to 1 mile. It shows the sidings which had been near the C of CLEVELEYS. From 1840 until 1851, the original track ran north almost straight from Burn Naze station, close to the river, on the wall sections shown. The terminus in that period was mid-way between the two northern stations seen here. The terminus from 1883 is shown as a rectangle adjacent to 'A585'. The engine shed is to the right of '15'.

Thornton Gate
Mineral Siding

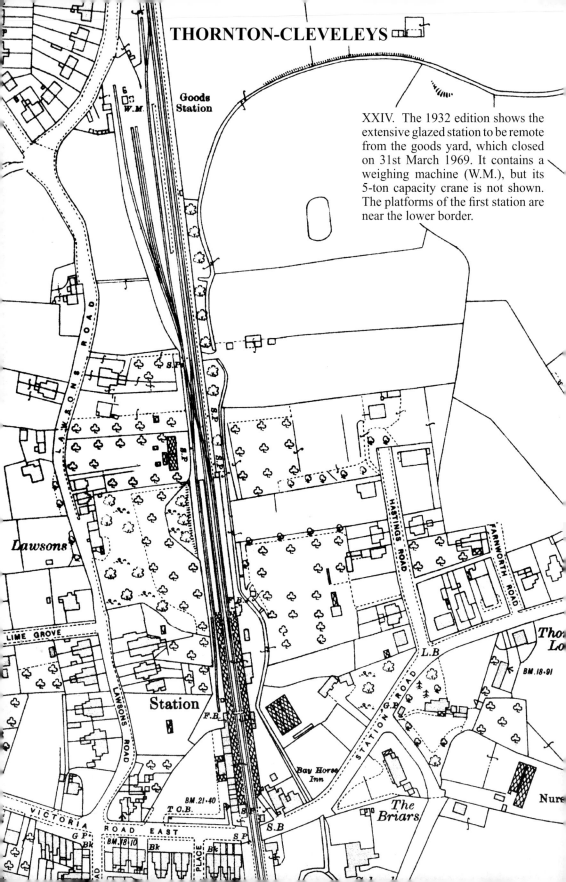

THORNTON-CLEVELEYS

XXIV. The 1932 edition shows the extensive glazed station to be remote from the goods yard, which closed on 31st March 1969. It contains a weighing machine (W.M.), but its 5-ton capacity crane is not shown. The platforms of the first station are near the lower border.

107. An 0-6-2T is northbound and is standing in the second station, which was in use from 1865 to 1925. It was called Cleveleys until 1st April 1905, when it became 'Thornton for Cleveleys', and finally 'Thornton-Cleveleys' in 1953. (P.Laming coll.)

108. The station masters house is also seen on the left of the previous picture. The passenger facilities are single storey, but the area termed 'Gentlemen' has no roof, the custom of the Victorian era. The first station was on this site and was in use in 1842-43. It was called Ramper Road. (P.Laming coll.)

109. The west elevation of the spacious 1925 building is seen with period transport operating route 13. The extent of the triangular station approach can be found on the map. (P.Laming coll.)

110. The station closed to goods on 31st March 1969, although it was coal only after 31st December 1968. It closed to passengers on 1st June 1970. The name became Thornton-Cleveleys in February 1953. Northbound is the irregular Speedlink trip working from Warrington to Burn Naze and back. The loco was no. 25181 and the date was 4th April 1985. The inward traffic was one tank of paraffin wax from Birkenhead to Burn Naze and six empty cement tanks returning from Kirkham to Earles Sidings. Kirkham was a temporary offloading point for cement while work was carried out at the cement terminal at Preston Deepdale. The Speedlink traffic ceased shortly after the date of this photograph. The line was then in use again from 1987 until 1999 for block trains of vinyl chloride monomer from Burn Naze to Barry Docks. (P.D.Shannon)

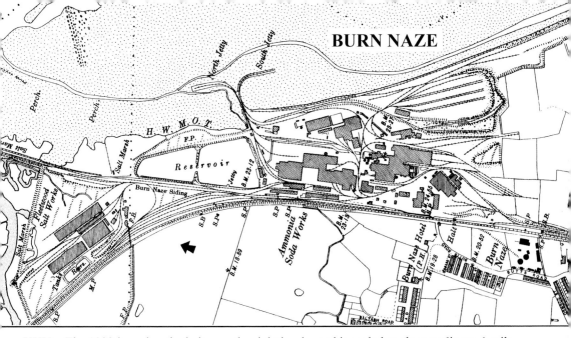

BURN NAZE

XXVa. The 1933 issue has the halt near the right border and is scaled at close to 6ins to 1 mile.

111. The small station opened on 1st February 1909 and lasted until 1st June 1970. The limited facilities are shown on a postcard. The poster board is headed L&YR and LNWR, which makes it prior to 1923. (P.Laming coll.)

XXVb. The diagram is from October 1990 and it shows the line northwards to Fleetwood as out of use. It closed in 1992, but the route south to Poulton-le-Fylde carried freight until 1996. (© TRACKmaps)

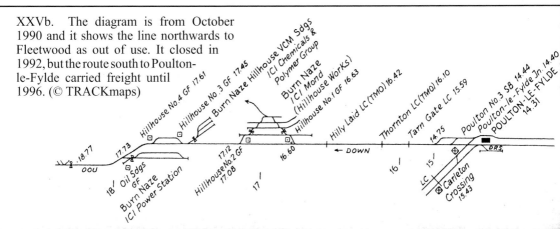

112. The bridge was built south of the station and it appears on map XXIII, along with more industrial development and sidings. The ticket office is now present at road level. Class 3 2-6-2T no. 40155 is seen on 10th August 1964. (C.J.Spring)

SOUTH OF WYRE DOCK

113. Not only has Blackpool the oldest electric tramway system in the world still running, but the only one never to close in England. Conduit electric cars operated by the Blackpool Electric Tramways Co Ltd started running in 1884. The line was taken over by the Corporation in 1892, extended in 1895 and 1897, and converted to overhead current collection in 1899. The Blackpool & Fleetwood Tramroad, eight miles long, was opened in 1898 by a company of that name between North Station and Fleetwood, reaching the seafront at Gynn Square. Blackpool's electric 'Steeple Cab' locomotive was built in 1927 by English Electric for towing coal wagons from a railway siding behind the Copse Road tram depot in Fleetwood to Thornton Gate sidings, 2½ miles away, where it is seen. The coal was for delivery by various coal merchants. The loco went to Crich Tramway Museum in 1966. Coal movement ceased in 1949, but the yard continued to be used for permanent way work and storage. It can be seen in picture 107 in the Middleton Press album *Blackpool Tramways 1933-66*. The power station and tram depot were also served by this loco. They were in Copse Road, to the west of Wyre Dock. (H.Nicol coll.)

114. The salt works was opened by the United Alkali Company in the 1890s and it later became part of Imperial Chemical Industries. No. 40155 is running into their sidings on 19th February 1980 with a short rake of caustic soda tanks, from Warrington. The last chemical tank trains ran from ICI Hillhouse at Burn Naze to Barry, in South Wales. (J.Matthews)

WYRE DOCK

115. The 6.53pm Preston to Fleetwood was recorded in July 1963, behind class 5 4-6-0 no. 45024. This station opened on 1st December 1885 for down trains and on 1st May 1901 for up. It was renamed FLEETWOOD on 18th April 1966 when it became a terminus, instead of the one seen in the remaining photographs. (Colour-Rail.com)

← XXVI. The 1933 survey has the engine shed lower left, Wyre Dock station at the northern corner of the dock area and the terminus top right. The scale is about 6ins to 1 mile and the main leisure area is top left. A lens helps to see many commercial details of interest. Their stories are complex. Notable was the provision of a slipway by the LMS in 1938. It was the biggest in Great Britain and could take 1050 tons. The connection between the tramway and the railway is semi-circular, left of centre. The former's terminus was at the top of the page, but the tracks to it are not shown; a rare omission. The ferry stage (top right) had been the end of the line from 1925. The tram stops are marked Sta. for Station. The main ones still have substantial brick-built waiting shelters.

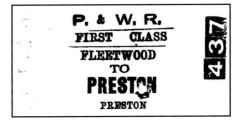

↙ Inset: The 1932 map, inset, has been reduced from 25ins to 1 mile to show the complete tram route, which was not shown on the 6ins survey, above.

116. This is the west elevation of the third station, which opened on 15th July 1883 and was photographed on 29th October 1966. It has since vanished. The second had been in Dock Street and was in use from 13th February 1841 until 1883. The first was nearby and lasted only eight months. The tram loop seen here came in 1925; until then trams terminated at Bold Street, shown at the top of the map. (Colour-Rail.com)

117. A policeman scans the departures with his back to platform 5. Knott End and Barrow were among many maritime destinations available from here. In November 1894, Bradshaw included Belfast and Londonderry. The Isle of Man was listed until 1961. Work to build Wyre Dock began in 1864 and the L&YR took it over in 1871. The Fish Dock was added in 1908, but fishing underwent a decline in the 1960s. The Stena Line sailed to Larne regularly in 2004-10. (P.Laming coll.)

118. Post-marked 1911, this card emphasised the town's main product and its promotional abilities. The same attribute continues more than a century later with 'Fisherman's Friends', which are produced nearby and marketed worldwide as an effective throat lozenge. The town expanded greatly in the first half of the 20th century with the growth of the UK fishing industry, to become a deep-sea fishing port. Decline of the industry began in the 1960s and it was hastened by the 'Cod Wars' with Iceland. Fish processing, however, remained a major economic activity. (P.Laming coll.)

119. A northward view from the footbridge shown on the map was recorded on 19th August 1959 and includes class 4 2-6-4T no. 80046. General goods traffic was discontinued on 18th April 1966, as were passenger services. These then terminated at Wyre Dock, which was renamed Fleetwood from that day until line closure to passengers in 1970. (Colour-Rail.com)

120. The engine shed is seen on 3rd October 1965 and on view are nos 84018, 45347 and 48338. The 1883 shed housed 33 locos in 1950. It was then coded 28B, later 24F and, finally, 10C. It closed on 14th February 1966 and was demolished in the mid-1980s. The end of BR steam in Lancashire came in August 1968. The population of the town rose from 12,082 in 1901 to 28,220 in 1961. (Colour-Rail.com)

MP Middleton Press

EVOLVING THE ULTIMATE RAIL ENCYCLOPEDIA

Easebourne Midhurst GU29 9AZ. Tel:01730 813169

www.middletonpress.co.uk   email:info@middletonpress.co.uk
A-978 0 906520 B- 978 1 873793 C- 978 1 901706 D-978 1 904474
E - 978 1 906008 F - 978 1 908174 G - 978 1 910356

All titles listed below were in print at time of publication - please check current availability by looking at our website - www.middletonpress.co.uk or by requesting a Brochure which includes our *LATEST RAILWAY TITLES* also our TRAMWAY, TROLLEYBUS, MILITARY and COASTAL series

A
Abergavenny to Merthyr C 91 8
Abertillery & Ebbw Vale Lines D 84 5
Aberystwyth to Carmarthen E 90 1
Allhallows - Branch Line to A 62 8
Alton - Branch Lines to A 11 6
Andover to Southampton A 82 6
Ascot - Branch Lines around A 64 2
Ashburton - Branch Line to B 95 4
Ashford - Steam to Eurostar B 95 4
Ashford to Dover A 48 2
Austrian Narrow Gauge D 04 3
Avonmouth - BL around D 42 5
Aylesbury to Rugby D 91 3

B
Baker Street to Uxbridge D 90 6
Bala to Llandudno E 87 1
Banbury to Birmingham D 27 2
Banbury to Cheltenham E 63 5
Bangor to Holyhead F 01 7
Bangor to Portmadoc E 72 7
Barking to Southend C 80 2
Barmouth to Pwllheli E 53 6
Barry - Branch Lines around D 50 0
Bartlow - Branch Lines to F 27 7
Bath Green Park to Bristol C 36 9
Bath to Evercreech Junction A 60 4
Beamish 40 years on rails E94 9
Bedford to Wellingborough D 31 9
Berwick to Drem F 64 2
Berwick to St. Boswells F 75 8
B'ham to Tamworth & Nuneaton F 63 5
Birkenhead to West Kirby F 61 1
Birmingham to Wolverhampton E253
Blackburn to Hellifield F 95 6
Bletchley to Cambridge D 94 4
Bletchley to Rugby E 07 9
Bodmin - Branch Lines around B 83 1
Boston to Lincoln F 80 2
Bournemouth to Evercreech Jn A 46 8
Bournemouth to Weymouth A 57 4
Bradshaw's History F18 5
Bradshaw's Rail Times 1850 F 13 0
Bradshaw's Rail Times 1895 F 11 6
Branch Lines series - see town names
Brecon to Neath D 43 2
Brecon to Newport D 16 6
Brecon to Newtown E 06 2
Brighton to Eastbourne A 16 1
Brighton to Worthing A 03 1
Bristol to Taunton D 03 6
Bromley South to Rochester B 23 7
Bromsgrove to Birmingham D 87 6
Bromsgrove to Gloucester D 73 9
Broxbourne to Cambridge F16 1
Brunel - A railtour D 74 6
Bude - Branch Line to B 29 9
Burnham to Evercreech Jn B 68 0

C
Cambridge to Ely D 55 5
Canterbury - BLs around B 58 9
Cardiff to Dowlais (Cae Harris) E 47 5
Cardiff to Pontypridd E 95 6
Cardiff to Swansea E 42 0
Carlisle to Hawick E 85 7
Carmarthen to Fishguard E 66 6
Caterham & Tattenham Corner B251
Central & Southern Spain NG E 91 8
Chard and Yeovil - BLs a C 30 7
Charing Cross to Dartford A 75 8
Charing Cross to Orpington A 96 3
Cheddar - Branch Line to B 90 9
Cheltenham to Andover C 43 7
Cheltenham to Redditch D 81 4
Chester to Birkenhead F 21 5
Chester to Manchester F 51 2
Chester to Rhyl E 93 2
Chester to Warrington F 40 6
Chichester to Portsmouth A 14 7
Clacton and Walton - BLs to F 04 8
Clapham Jn to Beckenham Jn B 36 7
Cleobury Mortimer - BLs a E 18 5
Clevedon & Portishead - BLs to D180

Consett to South Shields E 57 4
Cornwall Narrow Gauge D 56 2
Corris and Vale of Rheidol E 65 9
Coventry to Leicester G 00 5
Craven Arms to Llandeilo E 35 2
Craven Arms to Wellington E 33 8
Crawley to Littlehampton A 34 5
Crewe to Manchester F 57 4
Crewe to Wigan G 12 8
Cromer - Branch Lines around C 26 0
Croydon to East Grinstead B 48 0
Crystal Palace & Catford Loop B 87 1
Cyprus Narrow Gauge E 13 0

D
Darjeeling Revisited F 09 3
Darlington Leamside Newcastle E 28 4
Darlington to Newcastle D 98 2
Dartford to Sittingbourne B 34 3
Denbigh - Branch Lines around F 32 1
Derby to Chesterfield G 11 1
Derby to Stoke-on-Trent F 93 2
Derwent Valley - BL to the D 06 7
Devon Narrow Gauge E 09 3
Didcot to Banbury D 02 9
Didcot to Swindon C 84 0
Didcot to Winchester C 13 0
Dorset & Somerset NG D 76 0
Douglas - Laxey - Ramsey E 75 8
Douglas to Peel C 88 8
Douglas to Port Erin C 55 0
Douglas to Ramsey D 39 5
Dover to Ramsgate A 78 9
Drem to Edinburgh G 06 7
Dublin Northwards in 1950s E 31 4
Dunstable - Branch Lines to E 27 7

E
Ealing to Slough C 42 0
Eastbourne to Hastings A 27 7
East Cornwall Mineral Railways D 22 7
East Croydon to Three Bridges A 53 6
Eastern Spain Narrow Gauge E 56 7
East Grinstead - BLs to A 07 9
East Kent Light Railway A 61 1
East London - Branch Lines of C 44 4
East London Line B 80 0
East of Norwich - Branch Lines E 69 7
Effingham Junction - BLs a A 74 1
Ely to Norwich C 90 1
Enfield Town & Palace Gates D 32 6
Epsom to Horsham A 30 7
Eritrean Narrow Gauge E 38 3
Euston to Harrow & Wealdstone C 89 5
Exeter to Barnstaple B 15 2
Exeter to Newton Abbot C 49 9
Exeter to Tavistock B 69 5
Exmouth - Branch Lines to B 00 8

F
Fairford - Branch Line to A 52 9
Falmouth, Helston & St. Ives C 74 1
Fareham to Salisbury A 67 3
Faversham to Dover B 05 3
Felixstowe & Aldeburgh - BL to D 20 3
Fenchurch Street to Barking C 20 8
Festiniog - 50 yrs of enterprise C 83 3
Festiniog 1946-55 E 01 7
Festiniog in the Fifties B 68 8
Festiniog in the Sixties B 91 6
Ffestiniog in Colour 1955-82 F 25 3
Finsbury Park to Alexandra Pal C 02 8
French Metre Gauge Survivors F 88 8
Frome to Bristol B 77 0

G
Galashiels to Edinburgh F 52 9
Gloucester to Bristol D 35 7
Gloucester to Cardiff D 66 1
Gosport - Branch Lines around A 36 9
Greece Narrow Gauge D 72 2

H
Hampshire Narrow Gauge D 36 4
Harrow to Watford D 14 2
Harwich & Hadleigh - BLs to F 02 4
Harz Revisited F 62 8

Hastings to Ashford A 37 6
Hawick to Galashiels F 36 9
Hawkhurst - Branch Line to A 66 6
Hayling - Branch Line to A 12 3
Hay-on-Wye - BL around D 92 0
Haywards Heath to Seaford A 28 4
Hemel Hempstead - BLs to D 88 3
Henley, Windsor & Marlow - BLa C77 2
Hereford to Newport D 54 8
Hertford & Hatfield - BLs a E 58 1
Hertford Loop E 71 0
Hexham to Carlisle D 75 3
Hexham to Hawick F 08 6
Hitchin to Peterborough D 07 4
Holborn Viaduct to Lewisham A 81 9
Horsham - Branch Lines to A 02 4
Huntingdon - Branch Line to A 93 2

I
Ilford to Shenfield C 97 0
Ilfracombe - Branch Line to B 21 3
Industrial Rlys of the South East A 09 3
Ipswich to Diss F 81 9
Ipswich to Saxmundham C 41 3
Isle of Man Railway Journey F 94 9
Isle of Wight Lines - 50 yrs C 12 3
Italy Narrow Gauge F 17 8

K
Kent Narrow Gauge C 45 1
Kettering to Nottingham F 82-6
Kidderminster to Shrewsbury E 10 9
Kingsbridge - Branch Line to C 98 7
Kings Cross to Potters Bar E 62 8
King's Lynn to Hunstanton F 58 1
Kingston & Hounslow Loops A 83 3
Kingswear - Branch Line to C 17 8

L
Lambourn - Branch Line to C 70 3
Launceston & Princetown - BLs C 19 2
Leek - Branch Line From G 01 2
Leicester to Burton F 85 7
Leicester to Nottingham G 15 9
Lewisham to Dartford A 92 5
Lincoln to Cleethorpes F 56 7
Lincoln to Doncaster G 03 6
Lines around Stamford F 98 7
Lines around Wimbledon B 75 6
Liverpool Street to Chingford D 01 2
Liverpool Street to Ilford C 34 5
Llandeilo to Swansea E 46 8
London Bridge to Addiscombe B 20 6
London Bridge to East Croydon A 58 1
Longmoor - Branch Lines to A 41 3
Looe - Branch Line to C 22 2
Loughborough to Nottingham F 68 0
Lowestoft - BLs around E 40 6
Ludlow to Hereford E 14 7
Lydney - Branch Lines around E 26 0
Lyme Regis - Branch Line to A 45 1
Lynton - Branch Line to B 04 6

M
Machynlleth to Barmouth E 54 3
Maesteg and Tondu Lines E 06 2
Majorca & Corsica Narrow Gauge F 41 3
March - Branch Lines around B 09 1
Market Drayton - BLs around F 67 3
Market Harborough to Newark F 86 4
Marylebone to Rickmansworth D 49 4
Melton Constable to Yarmouth Bch E031
Midhurst - Branch Lines of E 78 9
Midhurst - Branch Lines to F 00 0
Minehead - Branch Line to A 80 2
Mitcham Junction Lines B 01 5
Monmouth - Branch Lines to E 20 8
Monmouthshire Eastern Valleys D 71 5
Moretonhampstead - BL to C 27 7
Moreton-in-Marsh to Worcester D 26 5
Morpeth to Bellingham F 87 1
Mountain Ash to Neath D 80 7

N
Newark to Doncaster F 78 9
Newbury to Westbury C 66 6
Newcastle to Hexham D 69 2

Newport (IOW) - Branch Lines to A 26 0
Newquay - Branch Lines to C 71 0
Newton Abbot to Plymouth C 60 4
Newtown to Aberystwyth E 41 3
Northampton to Peterborough F 92 5
North East German NG D 44 9
Northern Alpine Narrow Gauge F 37 6
Northern France Narrow Gauge C 75 8
Northern Spain Narrow Gauge E 83 3
North London Line B 94 7
North of Birmingham F 55 0
North of Grimsby - Branch Lines G 09 8
North Woolwich - BLs around C 65 9
Nottingham to Boston F 70 3
Nottingham to Lincoln F 43 7
Nuneaton to Loughborough G 08 1

O
Ongar - Branch Line to E 05 5
Orpington to Tonbridge B 03 9
Oswestry - Branch Lines around E 60 4
Oswestry to Whitchurch E 81 9
Oxford to Bletchley D 57 9
Oxford to Moreton-in-Marsh D 15 9

P
Paddington to Ealing C 37 6
Paddington to Princes Risborough C819
Padstow - Branch Line to B 54 1
Pembroke and Cardigan - BLs to F 29 1
Peterborough to Kings Lynn E 32 1
Peterborough to Lincoln F 89 5
Peterborough to Newark F 72 7
Plymouth - BLs around B 98 5
Plymouth to St. Austell C 63 5
Pontypool to Mountain Ash D 65 4
Pontypridd to Merthyr F 14 7
Pontypridd to Port Talbot E 86 4
Porthmadog 1954-94 - BLa B 31 2
Portmadoc 1923-46 - BLa B 13 8
Portsmouth to Southampton A 31 4
Portugal Narrow Gauge E 67 3
Potters Bar to Cambridge D 70 8
Preston to Blackpool G 16 6
Princes Risborough - BL to D 05 0
Princes Risborough to Banbury C 85 7

R
Railways to Victory C 16 1
Reading to Basingstoke B 27 5
Reading to Didcot C 79 6
Reading to Guildford A 47 5
Redhill to Ashford A 73 4
Return to Blaenau 1970-82 C 64 2
Rhyl to Bangor F 15 4
Rhymney & New Tredegar Lines E 48 2
Rickmansworth to Aylesbury D 61 6
Romania & Bulgaria NG E 23 9
Romneyrail C 32 1
Ross-on-Wye - BLs around E 30 7
Ruabon to Barmouth E 84 0
Rugby to Birmingham E 37 6
Rugby to Loughborough F 12 3
Rugby to Stafford F 07 9
Rugeley to Stoke-on-Trent F 90 1
Ryde to Ventnor A 19 2

S
Salisbury to Westbury B 39 8
Sardinia and Sicily Narrow Gauge F 50 5
Saxmundham to Yarmouth C 69 7
Saxony & Baltic Germany Revisited F 71 0
Saxony Narrow Gauge D 47 0
Seaton & Sidmouth - BLs to A 95 6
Selsey - Branch Line to A 04 8
Sheerness - Branch Line to B 16 2
Shenfield to Ipswich F 96 3
Shrewsbury - Branch Lines to A 86 4
Shrewsbury to Chester E 70 3
Shrewsbury to Crewe F 48 2
Shrewsbury to Ludlow E 21 5
Shrewsbury to Newtown E 29 1
Sierra Leone Narrow Gauge D 28 9
Sirhowy Valley Line E 12 3
Sittingbourne to Ramsgate A 90 1
Skegness & Mablethorpe - BL to F 84 0
Slough to Newbury C 56 7
South African Two-foot gauge E 51 2
Southampton to Bournemouth A 42 0
Southend & Southminster BLs E 76 5
Southern Alpine Narrow Gauge F 22 2
Southern France Narrow Gauge C 47 5
South London Line B 46 6
South Lynn to Norwich City F 03 1
Southwold - Branch Line to A 15 4
Spalding - Branch Lines around E 52 9

Spalding to Grimsby F 65 9
Stafford to Chester F 34 5
Stafford to Wellington F 59 8
St Albans to Bedford D 08 1
St. Austell to Penzance C 67
St. Boswell to Berwick F 44 4
Steaming Through Isle of Wig
Steaming Through West Ham
Stourbridge to Wolverhampto
St. Pancras to Barking D 68 5
St. Pancras to Folkestone E 8
St. Pancras to St. Albans C 7
Stratford to Cheshunt F 53 6
Stratford-u-Avon to Birmingh
Stratford-u-Avon to Cheltenh
Sudbury - Branch Lines to F
Surrey Narrow Gauge C 87 1
Sussex Narrow Gauge C 68 0
Swaffham - Branch Lines arou
Swanage to 1999 - BL to A 3
Swanley to Ashford B 45 9
Swansea - Branch Lines arou
Swansea to Carmarthen E 59
Swindon to Bristol C 96 3
Swindon to Gloucester D 46
Swindon to Newport D 30 2
Swiss Narrow Gauge C 94 9

T
Talyllyn 60 E 98 7
Tamworth to Derby F 76 5
Taunton to Barnstaple B 60 2
Taunton to Exeter C 82 6
Taunton to Minehead F 39 0
Tavistock to Plymouth B 88 6
Tenterden - Branch Line to A
Three Bridges to Brighton A 3
Tilbury Loop C 86 4
Tiverton - BLs around C 62 8
Tivetshall to Beccles D 41 8
Tonbridge to Hastings A 44 4
Torrington - Branch Lines to
Tourist Railways of France G
Towcester - BLs around E 39
Tunbridge Wells BLs A 32 1

U
Upwell - Branch Line to B 64
Uttoxeter to Macclesfield G 0

V
Victoria to Bromley South A 9
Victoria to East Croydon A 40
Vivarais Revisited E 08 6

W
Walsall Routes F 45 1
Wantage - Branch Line to D 2
Wareham to Swanage 50 yrs
Waterloo to Windsor A 54 3
Waterloo to Woking A 38 3
Watford to Leighton Buzzard
Wellingborough to Leicester
Welshpool to Llanfair E 49 9
Wenford Bridge to Fowey C 0
Westbury to Bath B 55 8
Westbury to Taunton C 76 5
West Cornwall Mineral Rlys D
West Croydon to Epsom B 08
West German Narrow Gauge
West London - BLs of C 50 5
West London Line B 84 8
West Wiltshire - BLs of D 12
Weymouth - BLs A 65 9
Willesden Jn to Richmond B
Wimbledon to Beckenham C
Wimbledon to Epsom B 62 6
Wimborne - BLs around A 97
Wirksworth - Branch Lines to
Wisbech - BLs around C 01 2
Witham & Kelvedon - BLs a F
Woking to Alton A 59 8
Woking to Portsmouth A 25 3
Woking to Southampton A 55
Wolverhampton to Shrewsbu
Wolverhampton to Stafford F
Worcester to Birmingham D 9
Worcester to Hereford D 38 8
Worthing to Chichester A 06
Wrexham to New Brighton F
Wroxham - BLs around F 31

Y
Yeovil - 50 yrs change C 38 3
Yeovil to Dorchester A 76 5
Yeovil to Exeter A 91 8
York to Scarborough F 23 9